Remembered with Pride

The stories of past pupils of the Hitchin Boys' British School who lost their lives in the Great War

Jean M. Handley

Jean M. Handley

28 . 6 . 14 .

A Hitchin Historical Society Publication

Remembered With Pride

A Hitchin Historical Society Publication 2014

© Jean M Handley and Hitchin Historical Society

ISBN: 978-0-9926162-0-5

Design, layout and photo enhancing: Barrie Dack and Associates
01462 834640

Printed by: Olive Press, The Green, Stotfold, Hitchin, Herts, SG5 4AN

Telephone 01462 733333

Inside front cover:	Street plan of Hitchin (The Official Guide 1921)
Half-title page:	The British Schools' Museum today
Frontispiece:	A typical soldier's kit c. 1916 photographed at Auchonvillers, Somme, France
Inside rear cover:	Temporary wooden crosses mark the graves
Back cover:	Author under the Menin Gate Memorial to the Missing, Ypres, Belgium, holding her late father's W.W.2 medals

www.britishschoolsmuseum.co.uk
www.hitchinhistoricals.org.uk

Contents

Just "a line" from **Hitchin.**

Foreword

One hundred years have elapsed since the start of 'The Great War' — 'The War to end all Wars', yet the awful (and aweful)ness of it and its enormity of scale still resonate down through the years. The waves of patriotism which swept throughout the United Kingdom and The Empire as hundreds of thousands of men answered the call to fight for King and Country (Conscription commenced in the Spring of 1916) did not pass by the small market town of Hitchin in rural Hertfordshire. As will be seen in this book, ex-pupils from Hitchin Boys' British School also went off to fight and alas, so many of them were destined never to return — some of the 10 million who died during those four years.

An author, when writing, always puts much more than just time, effort and money into the project but also part of one's inner self. This truism can be seen and felt here in Jean Handley's work. We met many years ago whilst I was a guide on her first battlefield tour and I was struck by her almost instant reaction to the historic events as they were unfolded. Her desire to know more has not diminished over the years during her many similar visits to many countries.

To put it at its most simplistic — she cares — deeply — and because of that, I am pleased and greatly honoured to be asked to write the foreword to this, yet another example of her excellent work. Four years of war followed by nearly four years of hard work and meticulous research into 'her boys' are encapsulated here where she has brought their family and military history to life.

It is to be hoped that some of the readers may be inspired to visit the battlefields and perhaps the fields and cemeteries where the fallen lie. Whether or not that be the case, the important thing is that they — and also those who fought and returned home, not all whole in mind and body — are not forgotten.

We Do Remember Them

Gordon Hall
Wollaston
Northants

Introduction

My interest in the Great War really started in 1997 when, after completing our family history back several centuries, my dear late father, himself a wounded WW2 soldier, commented, "That's all very well dear but I don't know what happened to my eldest brother who we think was killed in Gallipoli in W.W.1." This started me off on a whole new mission to find out more about Uncle William Benjamin Thomas Payne of the 1/4th Northamptonshire Regiment.

Hence a whole new world opened up. Family memories proved inaccurate as so often happens over time but 80 years on from his death in 1917 I was able to find out a great deal about Uncle William. He did in fact land in Gallipoli in 1915 but went on to fight in Palestine and was killed in April 1917 in the great battle of Gaza.

Research into family members' military details and friends' soldier relatives led me to join the Machine Gun Corps Old Comrades Association and with them I went on my first real battlefield tour. Since then I have been on a tour of Gallipoli and on over 20 trips to the battlefields of the Western Front. Research has become a passion, as I'm determined that the memories of those who fought and those who were lost, will not be forgotten.

Following this I have researched all the lads on my local war memorial (Sandon in Hertfordshire) plus those on three nearby villages, with more to go. Giving talks and putting my research into our local churches has enabled people to find out more about their soldier relatives and I hope I have inspired them to continue the quest. In 2004, as a result of many emotional visits, I put my own war poetry into print in my first book "Beacons of Remembrance" which has sold widely and is still available, with all the proceeds being donated to the Hitchin British Schools' Trust and the Royal British Legion.

Being involved at the British Schools' Museum since 1997 I resolved in 2010 to try to discover more about the pupils of the school who went off to that 'War to End all Wars' and did not return. I started by checking the internet for the Hitchin War Memorial website 'Lest We Forget' which gave me the names of all the local lads, plus some of their details. I then cross- checked these against our old school registers which proved to be the most difficult and painstaking job. I have proved as far as possible that 68 lads on the memorial came to our boys' school BUT I may be wrong and there could be more, but I cannot say with 100% certainty that that is the case. A good researcher has to be totally sure of the facts, so I will stick at 68. The school will be referred to as the Hitchin Boys' British School.

I have a great deal more information about each soldier than can be fitted into one book so I invite interested families to apply to me through the British Schools' Museum for extra details. I have taken all the photographs in the book, unless otherwise stated.

For each soldier, I have included the details from the admission register for the school, then I have thoroughly researched the census details of their families (on the 'Ancestry' website) that I hope will be a help to family historians. Readers will appreciate that whilst I have checked and re checked these, they do rely on census enumerators and transcribers in the past and cannot always be totally relied upon. Any addresses are in Hitchin, unless otherwise stated.

Next, the Commonwealth War Graves Commission website has been an invaluable first resource for checking details and getting me started with the military story of each lad. The Imperial War Museum's information in service records, pension records etc, obtained again through the 'Ancestry' website, has given me an illuminating insight into the lives of the combatants. 60% of the service records of soldiers from the Great War were lost in the 1940 bombing of The War Office repository in Arnside St. London in World War Two, so those that have survived, although rather burnt round the edges, I have been able to examine closely for more information. War diaries of some of the battalions are available and again they have revealed so much information to support my research and fill in the detail 'on the ground' of the last known positions of our soldiers. I say 'soldiers' because only 4 of our lads from land-locked Hitchin joined the navy but their stories have been really interesting too. None joined the Royal Flying Corps.

My vast library of military books (added to each birthday and Christmas by my generous husband) has been invaluable in my pursuit of the facts alongside the constant encouragement and expert help of my dear friend Gordon Hall whose knowledge of the period is encyclopaedic.

At this time I have personally visited 58 of the 68 graves or memorials and hope that it will be over 60 by the time of publication. Visiting the cemeteries, lovingly tended by the Commonwealth War Graves Commission, can be very sad but the sight of the care that they take in the beautiful planting is truly uplifting. When Sir Edwin Lutyens and Gertrude Jekyll planned these commemorative sites, her thoughts were that the shadow of an English rose should fall upon every grave at some point in every day. Roses certainly figure in many of the cemeteries but planting ideas have changed and all the sites/ cemeteries are colourful and meticulously mown.

These battlefield visits are always emotional journeys, for, over the period I have been involved in this research, the boys have become 'my boys' as I feel that I have got to know them and their families through the detail that I have unearthed. For quite a few I even have images of them, thanks to newspaper obituaries of the time. Many mention the letters received by the grieving parents that always talk about the bravery of the lads. If newspapers are referred to in the text they will be The Hertfordshire Express or the North Hertfordshire Mail of the period.

The Great War started for Britain on August 4th 1914 because of a complicated weave of treaties amongst European countries but was triggered by the assassination of the Archduke Franz Ferdinand of Austria in Sarajevo on June 28th 1914, the day I plan to launch this 'labour of love', 100 years on, in 2014. The following day, June 29th would have been my late father's 100th birthday and it is he that I thank for starting me on this quest and it is to his memory that I dedicate this book.

Jean M.Handley
June 2014

DEDICATION

To my father Cyril Payne
29-6-1914 — 2-10-2005

Photograph taken by Terry Ransome on 11.11.2004 at the launch of my
first book 'Beacons of Remembrance' at the British Schools' Museum

Acknowledgements

This book would not have been possible if had not been for three men in my life: my encouraging husband John, our dear friend and Great War expert, Gordon Hall and our close friend Peter Wignall who has been my patient, technical back-up man.

The lonely business of researching and writing has been greatly cheered by the information and the suggestions, insights and encouragement of so many individuals and friends.

Yvonne and the late Brian Limbrick M.B.E. encouraged me from the beginning, as have colleagues from the British Schools' Museum in Hitchin. I am indebted to Andy Gibbs, Terry and Rosemary Ransome, Jacky Birch, Fiona Dodwell (former curator), Valerie Marlow, Elizabeth Keech, Malcolm Parker, Stuart Antrobus, Angela Hillyard, John Pearce, Bill Wilson, Joy and Barry Hall, June and Terry Young, Annette Oliver, Betty Goble, Anne Wise (former manager), Mr Malcolm Brown, Headteacher and Mr Thomas Pitchford, Archivist at Hitchin Boys' School and so many others.

Supportive friends and relatives include Derek and Sue Fletcher, Kay Bolton, Marjorie Hall, Major Bill Jordan (R.E.M.E) Rtd., Chris and Joan Hoefkens, Robert and Christina Wornham, Jill and David Camps, Clive Harris (Battle Honours Ltd) and Trustees of the Western Front Association; Bruce Simpson, (Chairman) Colin Wagstaff, (Vice Chairman) Richard Hughes (Legal Officer) and John Richardson (Membership Officer).

Fellow researcher Steven Fuller's web site has been a great help with the Bedfordshire and Hertfordshire Regiments' war diaries. His work on transcriptions is admirable.

All photographs were taken by me except for the following for which I am very grateful.

All regimental badges were taken from Google Images on-line and cemetery plans and certificates were from the Commonwealth War Graves Commission. Newspaper photographs and advertisements from the North Hertfordshire Mail and the Hertfordshire Express of the period and the photograph of Thorpe's Yard were accessed in the Hitchin Museum, thanks to David Hodges and his staff. Bovington Tank Museum staff were very helpful and allowed me to use their archives on site.

I thank Susan Hamilton for the Day family photographs and information, Angela Hillyard and Keith Monk for the Farrow memorial plaque, Peter

Hawkins for the photograph of Arthur P. Hawkins, Brendan King for his King family photographs, Jonty Wilde for the photograph of soldier Abbiss and Jane Tunesi for the Ernest Morgan photographs. The Australian Archives on-line gave me access to the photograph of the Lechfeld P.O.W. cemetery funeral of George Young Lewis and his service records and the Canadian Military Archives on-line gave me access to Capt. Cecil Weare's service records.

The maps used are from my Naval and Military Press C.D. 'Trench Maps'. The maps of the Western Front and the Middle East were prepared by John Lucas for which I am very grateful. The service records, war medal index cards and census details were accessed on the 'Ancestry' website to which I have an annual subscription. All the black and white photographs were taken by me with permission at La Coupole Underground Exhibition, France. I am grateful to Jonty Wilde and Dan Hill (Herts at War project) for allowing me access to 'Hitchin's Century of Sacrifice', the early research by David Baines.

I am particularly grateful to the Hitchin Historical Society which, being a charity like the British Schools' Museum has worked in partnership with a common historical aim, to spread the word and remember the past. Their generosity in publishing the book and donating the profits to the British Schools' Museum is much appreciated. Derek Wheeler M.B.E. and Bridget and David Howlett did the meticulous and thorough proof reading exercise and were able to offer their special insights into military operations. John Lucas did a very professional job with the black and white maps for which I am also very grateful. Vicki Lockyer, of the Society will, I hope, be really busy with sales and distribution for which we are most grateful.

Barrie Dack has done a really professional job with the design and layout of my material and with such patience and good humour.

My *most* grateful thanks go to my expert publishing team, Scilla Douglas, Pauline Humphries and Yvonne Limbrick who, with endless patience, tolerance and cheerfulness have guided me through the final stages of getting the stories of *our boy*s into print.

THE GREAT WAR: A BRITISH PERSPECTIVE

In the decade after 1900 Europe was afflicted by rising international tensions that, several times, were defused just short of conflict. Focused mainly on Germany's growing assertiveness as a great power these tensions involved on one side the Kaiser and his close ally, Austria-Hungary, and on the other his rivals France, Russia and the United Kingdom. Even so, when hostilities actually erupted in August 1914, it was something of a surprise and few expected the war would last long. Almost until the last minute it was uncertain if the UK would act decisively in support of France and Russia but the German violation of Belgium's neutrality and civilian population ensured British forces were immediately committed to France.

A British Expeditionary Force (BEF) of about 90,000 regulars was despatched; by contrast France and Germany had, respectively, about 4 million and 5 million men under arms. Initial events in the west moved fast. British troops were quickly in action helping check the German advance. Equally quickly French and British (Allied) forces were pushed back. British troops played a key role in covering a retreat from Mons and Le Cateau; by November, after further hard fighting around Ypres, little of the BEF survived. In the east the Russians, recoiling from their defeat at Tannenberg, also failed to stem German success and, in October, Turkey declared war on the Allies. Germany lost its colonies in the Pacific (where Japan joined the Allies) and Africa, although in Tanganyika guerrilla resistance lasted to 1918. By the winter of 1914-15 fighting was solidifying, in the west, into the deadly stalemate of trenches, wire, mud, attrition, and 'no-man's-land' along a line from the Channel Coast to Switzerland that now encapsulates our view of the Great War.

Another 250,000 British troops were soon raised, mainly from the Territorials; volunteers also came from Britain's self-governing Dominions, from India and elsewhere in the Empire, setting a pattern for the rest of the war. Over the spring and summer of 1915 the Allies attempted to break the deadlock on the Western Front but failed, accruing major losses. There was new action in the Mediterranean. In April an Allied landing against Turkey was made at Gallipoli, famously including significant Australian and New Zealand (ANZAC) contingents; in May Italy joined the Allies and opened a front against Austria-Hungary. Gallipoli was costly and failed to break Turkey; ironically, the best organised aspect of the campaign was the swift withdrawal in the winter of 1915-16. The British also attempted to undermine Turkey

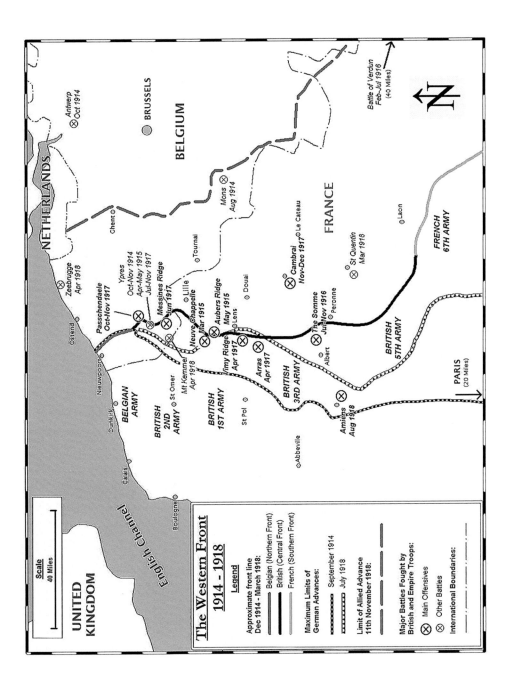

in Mesopotamia but this too ended in costly failure at Kut in April 1916. The British Government simultaneously faced a small but high profile Irish nationalist rebellion in Dublin.

The Royal Navy, unlike the BEF, was the most powerful in its class. It succeeded, despite a defeat at Coronel (off Chile) in November 1914 and the embarrassment of the shelling of some east coast ports in the winter of 1914-15, in countering the German surface fleet and establishing a blockade of its ports. Germany responded with a submarine campaign involving steadily more aggressive attitudes to merchant and non-combatant shipping. Notoriously, in May 1915, the British liner *Lusitania* was torpedoed without warning; over a hundred neutral Americans were among the dead. The huge German and British surface fleets, ironically a key focus of pre-war tensions, only engaged once in a major battle, in May 1916, at Jutland. British losses of men and ships were greater than those of the German fleet but the latter's resolve was broken. As a result, and facing a tightening Allied blockade, Germany redoubled its efforts in the submarine war.

Between February and July 1916 it was the Germans' turn to attempt a breakthrough on the Western Front by focusing on the French strong point of Verdun. British efforts to relieve pressure on the French sparked the battle of the Somme. A massive artillery bombardment preceded weeks of heavy fighting. On July 1st alone there were 60,000 British casualties and by October 1916 420,000 more casualties were sustained to achieve a seven mile advance along a thirty mile front. In the east the Russians made some progress against Austria-Hungary but the latter recovered as soon as German help arrived.

The cost of the land war to both sides was massive. Voluntary recruitment in the UK held up well but the demand for men was relentless. In January 1916, therefore, conscription was introduced in Great Britain. By early 1917 the Germans were reinforcing their positions with defence in depth, organised on the Siegfreid-Hindenberg Line. French and British forces responded with a new offensive but this stalled; the British achieved some success at Vimy Ridge near Arras in April but at a cost of another 142,000 casualties; many exhausted French troops mutinied. Between July and November 1917 another Allied push, including major tank deployments, culminated in the battle of Passchendaele which cost another 320,000 British casualties for little gain. If possible, the sense of hopeless deadlock was reinforced. The "industrialisation" of the conflict, including new uses of air power and Zeppelin raids on British civilians, was fully consolidated.

More widely the war went both badly and well for the Allies during 1917. Crucially Russia's support was eroded by internal crisis. In March the Tsar was deposed by liberals who, while continuing war against Germany, wanted peace; Russian resistance faltered in July allowing Austria to turn again on Italy. In

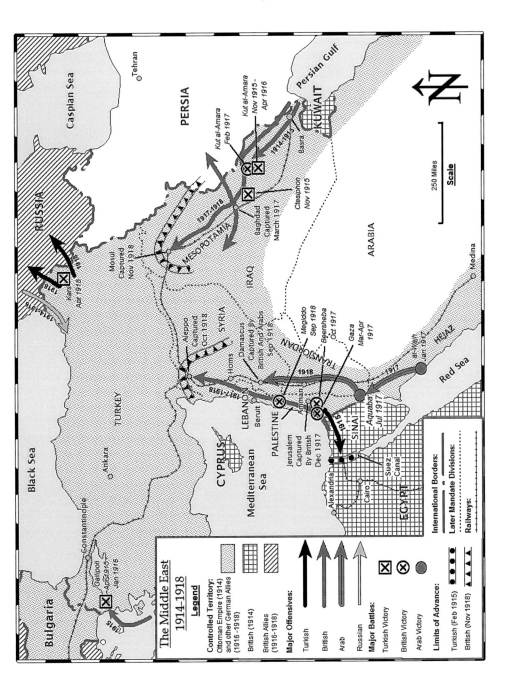

October the Russian liberals were, in turn, overthrown by Bolsheviks intent on seeking unilateral peace with Germany. More positively the United States, where anti-German feeling — epitomised by the *Lusitania* — was growing, declared war in April following the British release of the 'Zimmerman Telegram'. In this the Germans offered Mexico an offensive alliance against Washington. Additionally, the British made significant headway against the Turks by stirring an Arab Revolt and, in December 1917, capturing Palestine. Although it would be sometime before US forces reached Europe, and although the Turkish war was now something of a side-show, both contributed to a sense of at least some Allied progress. Germany concluded she must act before American troops and resources were fully engaged.

In March 1918, therefore, a new German offensive started in the west, just as the Bolsheviks concluded their separate peace of Brest-Litovsk. French and British forces remained weak after the losses of 1917 and, by May, German troops were within 40 miles of Paris. Continued German submarine success sparked rationing in Britain. The latest Allied crisis brought about unified Franco-British command and the first significant deployment of US troops. The Germans, overstretched and with increasing unrest at home, were checked and, in July 1918, also held on the Marne. The initiative at last passed to the Allies; by September, the Germans were in retreat following concerted pushes from French, British, Belgian and American troops.

The end came relatively quickly. By October 1918 Germany's government was crumbling, its High Seas Fleet mutinied and the Turks surrendered; in November a disintegrating Austria-Hungary also surrendered, the Kaiser abdicated and the German High Command decided war must end. Social tension was rising in all the major European combatants; exhaustion was symbolised by the virulent spread of Spanish flu. An Armistice was agreed with the Allies ending hostilities at 1100 on November 11th 1918; it was a German capitulation but no Allied troops had reached German soil. The costs of the war to Britain were monumental. Economic and financial strains had depleted long accumulated wealth at home and abroad and had very significantly increased national indebtedness. The human cost was unprecedented. British forces had enlisted about 9.5 million men, suffered about 950,000 deaths (about 750,000 from the UK and 200,000 from the Empire) and almost 2,150,000 wounded (about 1,750,000 from the UK and 400,000 from the Empire). For all combatants perhaps 10 million soldiers, and countless civilians, were killed. The cataclysm of the Great War, and the consequences of its peace concluded at Versailles, forged much of the modern world that we still live with today.

David Howlett

Hitchin Historical Society

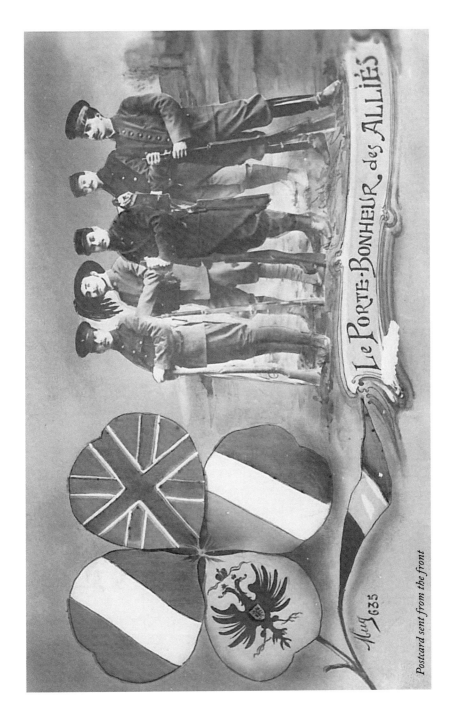

Le Porte-Bonheur des Alliés

Postcard sent from the front

6

HITCHIN IN 1914: A SNAPSHOT

With hindsight the Great War is a watershed often depicted as ending an Edwardian Golden Age of simpler values, security, prosperity and an apex of Britain's national power. What was Hitchin like on the eve of the conflict? Hitchin's medieval centre, just becoming recognised for its unique "historic character", functioned as the administrative, market, business and service focus for a wide area. The town's economy embraced agriculture, milling, brewing, tanning, pharmaceuticals, brick-making, construction and varied engineering. Hitchin's population of about 12,000 made it the largest urban centre in northern Hertfordshire.

It was the area's railway hub. Suburban growth, which had already seen spurts in the 1830s and after 1850, following the arrival of the railway, was now firmly underway with the piecemeal but steady spread of modest terraces to the north and northwest and much grander dwellings around The Avenue. The quality of life in these suburbs was improving with better housing, more material possessions, piped water, sewerage, and gas. A few families even had electric light and telephones and some of the bigger houses had novel "motor houses". The Cock Inn had just become the first local business to provide car hire. Hitchin's good railway service had spawned commuters. Improved opportunities for leisure included active sports, social and cultural clubs and new amenities such as the Blake Brothers' Picturedrome.

Hitchin's inhabitants had also benefited from considerable private philanthropy — from families such as the Wilsheres, Gainsfords and Seebohms — which enriched their religious, educational and social lives as well as aiding their health and well being. Continuity in local institutions, both public and private, was strong; town government was gradually taking on more and becoming increasingly democratic. The social reforms of the Liberal government at Westminster after 1906 heralded greater public intervention in individuals' lives; there were some immediate benefits such as the introduction of means tested old age pensions and National Insurance although the overall impact was still modest. The Hitchin Urban District Council's profile rose with a New Town Hall in 1901, a purpose built Fire Station in 1904, a Reservoir and Water Tower in 1909, planning for improved electricity supplies and better regulation of the general and cattle markets. Overall, at one look, the town could be seen as a relatively settled and prosperous community.

But there was also a darker side. Appalling slums, especially in Queen Street and in some town centre yards, housed those whom even modest prosperity had passed by. Like today, the town was at the mercy of wider economic pressures. Straw plaiting had faded under Chinese competition and, since the 1870s, Hertfordshire agriculture had been in varying stages of recession through poor seasons and cheap produce from abroad. Even better skilled jobs, such as in construction, metal working and engineering, were squeezed both by larger scale enterprises at home and by competitors abroad.

By 1914, real wages had stagnated for some time; those failing to make ends meet might well end up in the Hitchin Union Workhouse. There were worries that British innovation and enterprise were failing — foreign products abounded — and, despite the efforts of the UDC, there were still only six electric street lamps by 1914. Wider social and political pressures exacerbated a national sense of unease. Much of this passed Hitchin by as a country town but, for example, agitation for women's votes stimulated suffragette recruits and an Independent Labour Party branch was founded in 1908. Industrial unrest increased nationally and in 1911 Hitchin's railwaymen were affected by the first major coordinated stoppage in the industry.

Added to the mix were some very hot summers, two controversial General Elections in 1910, irritations of the wealthy over Liberal taxation policy, a mounting crisis in Ireland over Home Rule and tensions within Europe, which saw Hitchin's role as a local military centre reorganised. When war came on August 4th 1914, it was, however, still a shock. Hitchin's first trauma was a disturbance the day after, involving over 1,000 people, focused on Moss's grocery business: prices had gone up, panic buying began and popular resentment was immediate. The trouble was quickly defused but not before both the shop, and Mr Moss's house, were damaged — a tiny local harbinger of the stresses to come.

David Howlett

Hitchin Historical Society

SCHOOLDAYS

The registers record the dates of their entry to Hitchin Boys' British School for all those scholars destined to fight in, but not return from, the Great War. William Dimmock is the first of those entries, being admitted at 10 years of age in the year 1886, "in the time of the Great Fitch". Alderman Russell so described Mr. Fitch, highly respected Master of the Boys' School, who would have admitted William and collected from him the weekly school pence. As he walked along the muddy Queen Street, dodging the carts and horses rumbling along, young William would have entered the school premises on his best behaviour as he passed Mr. Fitch's front door and windows, to climb the slope to the Boys' School, sparks flying from his boots on the cobbled surface as he went.

His mother would have sent him in his fine white collar, folded over the lapels of his buttoned up jacket, trousers cut to the knee and his cap set straight upon his head, thus ensuring a neat and clean appearance for his inspecting teachers. He would have joined his friends on the playground, set at the top of the slope and right beside the monitorial Schoolroom.

Entering there, he would have been placed in one of the seven standards, each in charge of a certified teacher or pupil-teacher but all working in the same great Schoolroom under the sharp eye of the Master, Mr. Fitch who lived on site. With standards separated only by cupboards, the distractions must have been considerable!

When the youngest of our soldier heroes, George Ryall, registered in 1908, aged eight, he would have found things much changed. Mr. Fitch, accompanied on his last journey by almost the entire population of the town, anxious to pay their respects, had been laid to rest in Hitchin cemetery in St. John's Rd. Mr. Pengelly, the new Headmaster, was proving a worthy successor. George, like William before him, trudged up the slope but without so great a dread, Mr Pengelly having requested a larger house elsewhere in town.

At the top of the slope the old playground had disappeared beneath a new run of classrooms adjoining the Schoolroom with a study for the Headmaster abutting them. George would continue up the slope, clothed much as his predecessors had been, to the playground now located across Storehouse Lane, behind the Schoolroom. Mr. Pengelly, the Hertfordshire Express reported, "was a true friend to all the boys who passed through the school under him," so young George should have enjoyed a happy time there. He would most certainly

Mr Fitch,, wearing his distinctive top hat, with his teachers and pupil-teachers c.1890

have felt privileged since records note that, "it was the desire of the inhabitants of Hitchin that their children should be educated under Mr. Pengelly." This popularity and the fact that schooling was now free resulted in large classes, sixty pupils being quite the norm. The new building provided two light and airy classrooms furnished with new dual desks and seating a full complement of one hundred and twenty pupils between them. Four more classes were still accommodated in the Schoolroom and the Galleried classroom housed another. George's school was undoubtedly "buzzing!"

It is between these eras that all our schoolboy soldiers went to school. The leadership of inspirational Masters and the ideals they fostered, surely stood the boys in good stead on the battlefields, as it did in life. That so many acquitted themselves with honour, in the midst of the chaos that eventually claimed them, conjures up, in thoughtful times today, a special aura in their old classrooms.

They will be remembered there.

Yvonne Limbrick
British Schools' Museum

Boys stories

Arthur James Abbiss

Date of Birth: 19-7-1892
First School: Hitchin British Infants' School
Hitchin Boys' British School
Date of Admission: 29-5-1899
Parents: Frederick and Ellen
Address on admission: Union St [Oughtonhead Way]
Left school: 13-7-1906   Occupation: Milk boy

1901 Census details

In 1901 the family consisted of Father Frederick 41, a carpenter, (born in Holwell,) mother, Ellen 39, (born in Henlow) and their children, Ethel 17, John 13, Frederick 10, **Arthur** 8, Dora 5 and Ivy 3 who were all born in Hitchin. They were living at 8 Union Street.

1911 Census details

1 more child, Constance had been born (now 7 years) and the family of 7 were living in a 5 roomed house at 75 Tilehouse Street. The parents had married in 1882 and had 7 children still living.

Military details

Arthur joined the 11th Battalion Suffolk Regiment. He enlisted in March, Cambs. No. 13594 and was killed on the first day of the Battle of the Somme, July 1st 1916. The 11th (Service) Battalion (Cambridgeshire) of the Suffolk Regiment was part of 101 Brigade 34th Division. His medals entitlement shows that he did not reach France after training until the beginning of 1916. Corporal **Arthur Abbiss** and his comrades were brought up to Becourt Wood a few days before, ready for the July 1st attack. They were given their orders and told what the dress code was to be as the war diary extract below states.

Suffolk Regiment cap badge

All men to carry the following :
Rifle and equipment, 2 extra bandoliers of small arms ammunition, 2 Mills bombs, 1 Iron rations, 1 day rations, waterproof cape, 4 sandbags, 1 gas helmet and pair of goggles, 1 gas helmet pinned to shirt, a box respirator (for those who have one), a yellow triangle (inverted) on haversack, 1 pick or shovel, oil can and bottle, field dressing, no papers or orders apart from a 1/5000 German trench map.

Officers will carry a rifle and not a stick.

Cpl. Abbiss would have been mown down within moments of leaving his assembly position just south of the gigantic mine which was blown at 7.28am leaving the huge crater which is known as the Lochnagar Crater near the village of La Boisselle.

He was among 691 of his own battalion killed that day. He has no known grave and his name can be seen on the Thiepval

Lochnagar Crater, La Boiselle, France

Memorial to the Missing, Somme, France. Pier and Face 1C, and 2A. He was 23 years old.

Charles Marcus Barker

Date of Birth: 4-2-1883
First School: Hitchin British Infants' School
Hitchin Boys' British School
Date of Admission: 3-6-1889 Registered as Marcus Barker
Parents: William T. (a tailor) and Emily Barker
Address on admission: High Street
Left school: Possibly 1896   Occupation: ?

1891 Census details

The family was living at 14 High Street and consisted of William 47, a tailor (born in Cambridge), his wife Emily 44, (born in London), Emily Rose 17, William Charles 16, a tailor's apprentice, Frank 14, Albert 10, **Charles Marcus** 8, Herbert 3, all born in Hitchin, Harold Lawes 8, (nephew) and William Symonds, a boarder and tailor's apprentice.

1901 Census details

His name now appears as **Marcus** who at 18 is living with his uncle Frederick George Barker 47, (born in Hitchin), an ironmonger at The Green, Southgate, North London. **Marcus** was his assistant ironmonger.

1911 Census details

Marcus is now back in Hitchin aged 28, living with his widowed mother 64 and 3 siblings. He is recorded as a cutter/manager in their tailor's shop where mother was named as the shopkeeper and the siblings were all working in the business. They were living at 27 Nightingale Road.

Military details

Marcus enlisted in April 1916 and according to the *Herts Express* report of December 22nd 1917, this was to enable his brother H.E. Barker (Herbert was 5 years younger) to remain behind to run the family business in the Starling's Bridge area of Hitchin. **Marcus** joined the Machine Gun Corps as number 38195, later he was corporal 201484 in the Tank Corps in tank "G7"(named Giggle). Each

'Female' tank in action with the Canadians, Vimy Ridge April 1917

tank battalion was given a letter and the tanks were named appropriately eg, Goliath, Glenlivet, Grantham and Gondolier. **Marcus** would have been part of a crew of 8 in what was called a Mark 1V 'female tank'. This was armed with 6

Rare WW1. 'splatter' mask worn in tanks

machine guns and supported the advancing infantry whereas the 'male tanks' had heavier guns and led the advance. Conditions in the tanks were horrific and their crews' protective gear was inadequate for the heat and potential metal blast injuries.

He was killed in the big tank battle in November 1917 on the 23rd the third day of the battle, near the town of Cambrai, France. The tanks slowly ran out of power and got stuck in the mud, giving the enemy a chance to retaliate but the general advance lasted for 8 days, at the end of which we had taken some 10,000 prisoners and seized some 200 guns and moved right up to Bourlon Wood. To this day in hot, humid conditions, gasses still rise up there after nearly 100 years.

As he has no known grave Cpl.**Charles Barker** is commemorated on the Cambrai Memorial at Louverval, Nord, France, Panel 13. He was 34.

Harold Barker (cousin of Raymond Robinson)

Date of Birth: 7-10-1900
First School: St Saviour's Infant, Radcliffe Road
Hitchin Boys' British School
Date of Admission: 6-5-1907
Parents: Alfred (a wheelwright) and Alice
Address on admission: 2 Cambridge Road
Left school: ?   Occupation: ?

1901 Census details

The family was living at 6 Marshall Road, Cherry
Hinton, Cambs. Alfred 32, was a coachbuilder
(born in Braughing, Herts.) and his wife Alice was
also 32, (born in Barley, Herts.). They had **Harold**
6 months, who was born in Cambridge and a niece,
Edith Barker was there too, aged 14.

Queen's Royal West Surrey Regiment cap badge

1911 Census details

The family was now recorded as living at 2 Cambridge Terrace where Alfred
42, was a wheelwright. Alice was now 42, **Harold** was 10 and others had been
born. Stanley was 9, Alfred 8 and Alice 6, (all born in Cambridge). Little Olive
was 2 and had been born in Hitchin, suggesting that the family moved to the
town after 1905. The couple had been married for 12 years and had a five-
roomed house.

Military details

Harold had a close friend George Ryall. They
had been at school together, joined the Boy
Scouts together and entered the employment
of Messrs. G.W. Russell and Sons (leather
dressers) 74 Bancroft, but later Harold went
into the employment of Messrs. P.H. Barker
and Son.

The two boys enlisted together on October
23rd 1918, in Bedford in the same regiment.
They joined the 53rd (Young Soldier) Battalion
Queen's Royal West Surrey Regiment.
Harold, as private TR/161734, he never went
abroad. Sadly this young man died of influenza
aged 18 in hospital at St Albans where he was
stationed, just one week before the Armistice,

Harold's grave

on November 4th 1918 and is buried in Hitchin Cemetery (W.165) and remembered on the family grave there too. (S.section) The newspaper report gives details that his close friend George, died the day after in the same hospital. In death undivided.

Walter Bath

Date of Birth: 1-7-1884
First School: Walsworth
Hitchin Boys' British School
Date of Admission: 5-6-1893
Parents: James and Alice
Address on admission: 3 Willian Road, Walsworth
Left school: 24-7-1897   Occupation: ?

1891 Census details

The family was living at 4 Midland Cottages. James was 34 and working for the Great Northern Railway. Alice was 29 both having been born in Bedfordshire. Their children were Ralph 8, **Walter** 6, William 4, Lewis 2 and Noel 9 months. They'd moved between St Neots, Bradford and Hitchin throughout the births of these children and according to the admissions register for our Boys' School, they lived at 4 addresses in Hitchin when their children were registered between 1893 and1903! Poor Alice!

1901 Census details

They were living at Grove Road. Another son, Fordham had appeared aged 16, so he was obviously elsewhere at the time of the 1891 census. Unlike the other boys who worked for the railway like father, he worked in a timber yard. Alice had had another child, Harold now 4. **Walter** was not at home but further research showed that he had joined the army.

1907

Walter married Ada Wilshere, the daughter of James and Harriett Wilshere.

In the 1901 census her parents were 55 and 56. James was a railway ballast labourer and Harriett was a home-based straw plaiter at 13 Sunnyside. Their children were Ada 16, Fred 11, Willie 9 and granny, Louise Wilshere at 75, a widow, was living with them.

1911 Census details

Walter was now 26 and Ada 24. They were living in 5 roomed accommodation at 11 Cannon's Cottages, Sunnyside. They'd been married for 4 years and he was a railway labourer but, because on this census the head of household filled in his own details, it was obvious that Walter had been taught well as his handwriting was very clear!

Military details

Miraculously, Walter's service records have survived though they are very burnt round the edges!

From the details it can be concluded that:

☆ He joined the army on April 2nd 1902 aged 18 years 7 months and chose the Rifle Brigade. He was given the number 8979.

☆ He was medically examined at Bedford where his height, weight and complexion were recorded on April 3rd.

☆ Posted July 9th 1902 to S.Africa for clearing up operations, the 2nd Boer War having ended in May 1902.

☆ Returned February 3rd 1903 to England.

☆ Between May 21st 1903 and June 2nd 1904 he was confined to barracks 11 times for incidents varying from being drunk, being absent from parades and having a dirty rifle. These incidents it seems, took place in London.

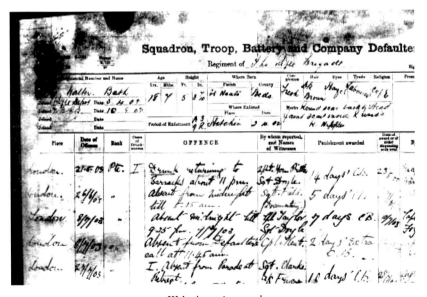

Walter's service record

☆ He left the army 196 days after his return from Africa according to the records but remained in the Army Reserve.

☆ October 25th 1913 he re-engaged for section D. Army Reserve for a further 5 years (or longer should the country be in a state of war).

☆ This happened in 1914 and he was mobilized in August and left for Le Havre as part of the 1st Battalion, 11th Brigade, 4th Division landing on August 23rd.

The records show that 'on September 7th 1914 he was hospitalised with indigestion and (?) but re-joined his unit on 23/9 at Le Cart?' [sic]

Then on February 16th 1915 he was given a 14 day Field Punishment no. 1 for 'Disobedience of orders whilst on sentry duty, allowing civilians to enter the billet'. This was indeed harsh, as detailed below.

Field Punishment No. 1 comprised a British Army punishment imposed for minor offences such as drunkenness and was often applied during the First World War. A most humiliating form of punishment which continued into the late 1920s, it saw the soldier in question attached standing full-length to a fixed object, either a post or a gun wheel, for up to two hours a day (often one hour in the morning and another in the afternoon) for a maximum of 21 days. An earlier punishment by flogging had been abolished within the British Army in 1881.

Stories abound of soldiers positioned to face the enemy lines, invariably out of range of enemy fire but allegedly not always so. If exposed to open sunshine this form of punishment proved even more discomforting, quite aside from the constant problem of trench lice. If the soldier in question started to sag while attached to the post he would often be checked by military police.

Walter's 4th Division was involved in various battles in late 1914 like the Aisne, Armentières and Messines then in 1915 the battles of Ypres including St Julien, Frezenberg Ridge and Bellewaarde Ridge from April 25th to May 25th.

The Menin Gate, Ypres, Belgium

On May 2nd the Division was holding the line between Gravenstafel and Turco Farm (near the village of St Julien) when the Germans launched yet another gas attack - having done so a few times earlier after April 24th when they launched their first. This time it was on a three mile front. The chlorine gas came across at about 4.30 pm. having been preceded by a heavy explosive artillery barrage. The German infantry then carried out later attacks but were repulsed. On May 4th 1915 the line was stabilised and the enemy got no further towards Ypres.

Rifleman **Walter Bath** was killed in action aged 30 on May 3rd 1915 and is commemorated on the Menin Gate Memorial to the Missing in Ypres, Panels 46-48, as he has no known grave.

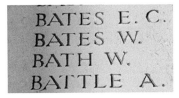

Ada his wife was given 10 shillings a week as a pension because in total he had completed 13 years and 32 days of army service.

Named on the Menin Gate

Horace Leonard Bavington

Date of Birth: 17-2-1896
First School: Hitchin British Infants' School
Hitchin Boys' British School
Date of Admission: 1-5-1902
Parents: William (a carter) and Harriett
Address on admission: 8 Queen Street
Left school: 17-2-1910   Occupation: Errand Boy

1891 Census details

The family was living at 47 Queen Street. William 26 (born in Newport Pagnell), was a coal porter and his wife Harriett was also 26. They had William 4 and Arthur 2.

1901 Census details

At this time they were living at 47 Queen Street near the King's Head public house. William was now a bricklayer for G.N.Railway. Young William now 14, was a distiller's bottle washer and **Horace Leonard** 5, Harold 3 and Elsie, 1 month, had increased the size of the family.

1911 Census details

This shows them living at 72 Queen Street and William was a wood sawyer. The couple had been married for 24 years. William junior was a labourer at the distillery, **Horace Leonard** aged 15, was a butcher's errand boy with the Premier Meat Company at 3, The Market Place and Harold, Elsie and Lilian were pupils at the British Schools. They were living in a 6 roomed home and Mr Bavington who filled in the census form, wrote beautifully!

Military details

The military records of this soldier have miraculously partially survived.

☆ **Horace** enlisted on March 10th 1913 aged 17 for service in the Territorial Force of the 1st Battalion Herts Regiment for 4 years as Pte.2145 (which changed to 265306 on February 24th 1917) He was living at 96 Nightingale Road and was working for the Great Northern Railway as a clerk.

☆ He was declared medically fit on March 14th 1913 where his weight, height and eye colour was recorded. During the next year he would have had regular drills at a local drill hall and been to at least one summer camp.

☆ When war broke out the following year he was 'embodied' on August 5th 1914 but did not leave for France until January 20th 1915 after further training. (He was in France from then until July 24th 1917).

☆ On January 23rd 1915 he suffered from inflamed tonsils but re-joined his unit on February 4th 1915.

☆ He was made an acting Lance Corporal on May 30th 1915.

☆ Then on July 3rd 1915 he was admitted to a field ambulance station with a fever for 6 days.

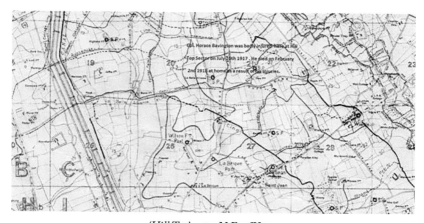

'Hill Top' sector. N.E. of Ypres

☆ He rose to the rank of corporal on September 11th 1916
☆ It is recorded that he was awarded a Distinguished Conduct Medal (London Gazette January 26th 1917)

For conspicuous gallantry in action.

He led a bombing party with great gallantry and rendered valuable assistance in the consolidation of the position. He has at all times set a splendid example.

☆ He was wounded on May 7th 1917 when his mother was recorded as living at 5 Anchor Cottages, Walsworth.
☆ Then on or about July 10th 1917 he was badly wounded near Ypres in Belgium. The Regimental War Diary shows the battalion was relieving the 1st Cambridgeshire Regiment in the front line system at Hill Top Sector between 7th and 16th so it can be concluded that this is where he was hit by shrapnel. After an operation on July 16th 1917 at the Front (trepanning took place to relieve pressure on the brain on the left side) he was evacuated to England on July 24th 1917.
☆ The medical report from Croydon War Hospital where he was sent from the Front describes terrible injuries sustained whilst in the trenches. *He had a scar above the left eyebrow where a drainage tube had been inserted and where 'brain substances' had been leaking for 6 weeks. The left eye had*

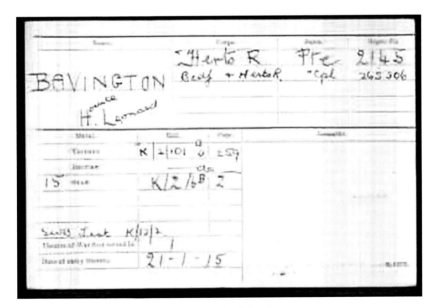

His Medal Rolls Card

been excised and part of the left frontal bone had gone, including the orbital plate. There was a distinct pulsation of the brain over the left frontal region. The left socket still discharged slightly. X-ray showed a small metal fragment lying on the right plate bone, which, it was said caused no disability. He was deaf in the left ear but had no limb paralysis.

☆ A medical board confirmed him *'fit for discharge'* on October 9th 1917, after 4 years and 214 days service. With a Chelsea pension number of 131373 he was to receive 30 shillings a week from October 10th 1917 to November 6th 1917 then 24 shillings a week from November 7th 1917 to November 5th 1918 with an added 6d. per day because he had been awarded the D.C.M. He lived then at 5 Anchor Cottages with his mother.

Cpl. **Horace Bavington** died as a result of his horrific injuries less than 3 months later on February 21st 1918 just 4 days after his 22nd birthday. He was buried in Hitchin Cemetery N.E. extension, grave 573. The family's inscription was 'Asleep'. His regiment had seen action in all the major battles of the war including Loos, the Somme and Vimy Ridge. *What a sad loss.*

W. L. Welsh, R.N.A.S., in the Western theatre of war on July 14.

HITCHIN D.C.M. HERO WOUNDED.

Corporal H. L. Bavington, Herts. Regiment, son of Mr. and Mrs. Bavington, of Walsworth, who won the D.C.M. just after Christmas for bravery on the Somme, has been seriously wounded in the head, resulting in the loss of the left eye. He received the wound on going back at the end of his recent leave.

Corporal Bavington was a member of the Herts. Territorials, and after mobilisation went to France with them in 1914. He was 21 years of age last February.

ACTING-LIEUTENANT NOEL BROWNING WOUNDED.

Herts Express report July 1917

Herbert Edward Brandon

Date of Birth: 17-7-1897
First School: Hitchin British Infants' School
Hitchin Boys' British School
Date of Admission: 2-5-1904
Parents: Frederick (gardener) and Sarah Emily
Address on admission: Priory Gates
Left school: 3-8-1911 Occupation: Clerk

1901 Census details

The family was living at Priory Gates and Frederick 32, (born in Tring) was a gardener, presumably at the Priory. He and his wife Sarah Emily 35 had 4 children, George W. 7, Frank F. 6, **Herbert E.** 4 and Annie E.1.

1911 Census details

Sadly Emily is now a widow and in the Hitchin Union workhouse aged 45. She had been married for 18 years and it appears had had 7 children, 5 of whom were still living.

Annie Elizabeth 11 and Sidney (born January 21st 1903) were living in the Letchworth childrens home at 28-32 Ridge Road, Letchworth. George 16 and Frank 15 were now boarding at 57 Bunyan Road at the home of George and Elizabeth Day. George was a gardener and Frank a fitter (Engineering).

Herbert cannot be found in this census.

Military details

Stoker 2nd Class **Herbert Brandon** was on SS/116773 HMS Lilac in the Royal Navy when he was killed on August 18th 1915 in the incident outlined below. He is commemorated on Panel 12 of the Chatham Naval Memorial. He was only 18 years old.

Chatham Naval Memorial

HMS Lilac had recently joined our Grand Fleet as part of a minesweeping flotilla. On the 18th of August, 1915. Lt. Commander L. Fisher was sweeping the Meteor-laid minefield in the Cromarty Firth. It was bad weather with a heavy sea running. Her stem [midship] hit a mine and her bows were blown off nearly as far as the bridge, with the remains hanging down from her keel. She was now drawing nearly 30 - 40 feet of water. She was towed by her sister ship Hollyhock into Peterhead where she received a new bow and rejoined the flotilla some months later. 16 ratings, including Herbert, were lost in this incident.

Edward Henry Briston

Date of Birth: 24-5-1898
First School: Hitchin British Infants' School
Hitchin Boys' British School
Date of Admission: 1-5-1905
Parents: Richard and Ellen
Address on admission: 55 Hitchin Hill
Left school: 23-5-1912   Occupation: Errand Boy

1901 Census details

Richard Henry 41, a blacksmith (born in Downham, Norfolk) with his wife Ellen 42 (born in Hitchin) was living at 55 Hitchin Hill with their 4 children. These were Jane G. 7, Beatrice 4, **Edward H. 2** and John W. 5 months.

1911 Census details

The family was now living at 35 Hitchin Hill. **Edward 13,** was at the British School. Father Richard was recorded as a 'shoeing smith' and had been married to Ellen for 18 years. The family was living in 4 rooms.

When **Edward** left school we know from the press reports that he was an assistant scoutmaster with the St Mary's troop and also a Sunday school teacher and member of the choir at St John's Church, formerly in St John's Road.

Military details

Edward enlisted in Bedford as 37591 in the 2nd Battalion Bedfordshire Regiment in 'B' company on January 27th 1917.

He went over to France after brief training on June 6th and had 14 days leave in February 1918 when he returned to Hitchin.

He died of wounds on July 2nd 1918 aged just 20 in the action described below in the Bedfordshire War Diary where his name is mentioned. This is quite unusual as generally only officer casualties were named.

Rev. Tilson sent a letter to his grieving parents telling them that their boy **Edward** was taken into Casualty Clearing Station No. 4 early on July 2nd having been badly wounded on June 30th and never rallied. He was given a Christian burial in the Pernois British Cemetery adjoining the hospital, the clergyman said.

Newspaper report
July 20.1918

From the war diary:

The Commanding Officer regrets to announce the following Casualties on 30th June, 1918. WOUNDED IN ACTION "A" Company 49675 Pte.H.Freeman [Harry FREEMAN], 39758 Pte.J.Stammers [James STAMMERS], 25841 Pte.A.Hilliard [Arthur HILLIARD], 49635 Pte.H.J.Henley [Henry J. HENLEY]. "B" Company 17956 Pte.E.Albon [Edward ALBON, MM], 25230 Pte.H.Bird [Horace BIRD], 413528 Pte.H.Burn [Harold BURN], 37591 Cpl.E.H.Briston [Edward H. BRISTON]' and many other casualties were recorded in the war diary.

ACCOUNT OF OPERATIONS AT BOUZINCOURT SPUR 30TH JUNE to 3RD JULY 1918

At 9.35 pm on the 30th June the 2nd Bedfordshire Regiment, in conjunction with the 12th Division on left and 6th Northamptons on right attacked the enemy trenches on the BOUZINCOURT SPUR N.W. of ALBERT. The attack was carried out by "B" Company under Lieut. H.B.Stewart [Hew Bertram STEWART, MC], with "C" Company under Lieut.K.J.Ritchie [Kenneth James RITCHIE], responsible for wiring the captured line and one platoon of "A" Company Carrying Party. "A" Company (less one Platoon) and "D" Company were in reserve in MELBOURNE TRENCH. The attack was carried out under a smoke screen and Stokes Barrages and was entirely successful, all objectives being gained, a large number of the enemy killed, three Machine Guns captured and about 20 prisoners taken. In addition Lieut. W.S.Oliver-Jones with a small party of men successfully bombed a number of dug-outs in the sunken road which were full of the enemy. Actual casualties during the assault were about one Officer 35 Other Ranks. Owing to enemy heavy artillery and Machine Gun fire "C" Company were unable to get any wire out and a Counter-Attack made by the enemy at 2.0 am on 1st July succeeded in driving in our most advanced posts. At 7.30 am a Counter Attack organised by Lieut. H.B.Stewart [Hew Bertram STEWART, MC] in conjunction with the 6th Queens on the left succeeded in regaining these posts but they were again lost at 4.30 pm after a long bombing contest. At 8.50 pm the enemy delivered a heavy counter attack on the whole front and succeeded in driving in the 12th Division on our left from their advanced position. "B" Company however held fast and at 2.0 am on the 2nd July they were relieved by "D" Company under Captain Reiss MC MM. [Phillip Julius REISS, MC & Bar, MM] A quieter day followed but at 9.25 pm after two hours heavy shelling, in the course of which the enemy obliterated a large portion and knocked out two Lewis Gun teams, the enemy attacked under a very heavy 5.9" barrage and succeeded in recapturing their original front line In spite of a magnificent resistance put up by a party under Captain Reiss and Lieut.Hughes. The total Casualties during the attack were 7 officers and 146 Other Ranks. The following immediate awards were received for this action: - Captain P.J.Reiss MC MM [Phillip Julius

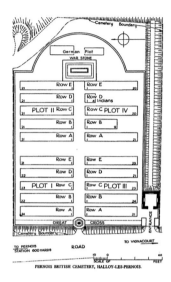

C.W.G.Certificate   *Plot 2, Row C. Grave 9*

REISS, MC & Bar, MM] BAR TO MILITARY CROSS **Lieut H.B.Stewart** *[Hew Bertram STEWART, MC] MILITARY CROSS* **Lieut.W.S.Oliver-Jones** *MILITARY CROSS No.10731 Sergt. Clarke C.* **[Charles CLARKE, DCM]** *"B" Company. D.C.M. No.17442 Pte.Goodliffe A. MM [Albert GOODLIFFE, DCM, MM & Bar] "B" Company D.C.M.* **L.H.Keep** *[Leslie Howard KEEP, DSO, MC] Major for Lt.Colonel Commanding 2nd Battalion Bedfordshire Regiment*

During May, June and July, the Division (18th) held the line opposite Albert. There was much patrol work and a few minor raids and the 54th Brigade (his), in particular made a serious effort to oust the Germans from the defences at the north-west corner of Albert, known as the "hairpin" system. Generally speaking, both sides were testing each other's strength, preparing for the great battles that were to set the world ablaze later in the year (8th August onwards) as we forced the enemy back during 'The Last 100 days' - 'The Advance to Victory'. The enemy launched their last big attack on the 4th April 1918 and on occasions got across the river Ancre, north of Albert and at the bottom of the slope below Bouzencourt. They were always fought off and never got to Bouzencourt village.

Cpl. Edward Henry Briston is buried in Pernois British Cemetery, Halloy-les-Pernois, Somme plot II, row C, grave 9.

Frank Brown

Date of Birth: 11-8-1884
First School: The National School, Preston [near Hitchin]
Hitchin Boys' British School
Date of Admission: 4-3-1895
Parents: Frank (Labourer) and Emma
Address on admission: Charlton
Left school: 1-5-1897   Occupation: ?

1891 Census details

The family was living at Sootfield Green, Preston. Father Frank 30, an agricultural labourer and Emma 32, had William 11, Sarah 9, Henry 8, **Frank 7**, Anna 5, Henrietta 4, Thomas 2 and Katie 6 months. They were recorded as having been born in Offley.

1901 Census details

They were now living in Hitchin at 3 Sharp's Yard. 2 more children had arrived, Jack 10 and Fred 3. Our **Francis Frank** (as he was now recorded) was 17 and a general labourer.

He married in 1904.

1911 Census details

Recorded as 25 and a farm labourer, he had been married for 7 years to Fanny Frances, 26 and they had Lily 6 and Reuben Walter 2. They were living at Charlton Cottages.

Military details

Frank enlisted in 1914 and joined the Bedfordshire Regiment as 17297 in 'B' Company, 8th Battalion. He went out to the battlefields after training on August 30th 1915 according to his medal entitlement card, so his wife would have received the 1915 Star, the War and Victory medals as well as the Memorial Plaque (often called the Dead Man's Penny) after his death on April 19th 1916.

The war diary gives the following information.

The enlisted men from all over the county mustered at their local train stations and were transported en-masse to the Regimental HQ at Bedford to be mobilised into the 8th Battalion of the Regiment. Other than a brief spell in Brighton, most of their training was undertaken in Surrey, with almost seven months being spent in the sprawling New Army training area around Woking.

Finally, the increasingly restless men of the 'Hungry 8th' (a nickname used in a letter home from Private 19861 Leslie Worboys) received orders to mobilize and prepared to ship out. At 11pm on the 28th August 1915, the Battalion boarded the troop trains at Chobham Station and left for Dover. After transferring straight onto troop ships, they arrived at Boulogne early on August 30th 1915.

Six weeks after landing in France, on October 11th 1915, the entire 71st Brigade was transferred into the 6th Division, which was a veteran Regular Army Division that had been serving in France since 1914. During another reorganisation on 17th November 1915, the battalion were transferred to the 16th Brigade of the 6th Division.

The 8th battalion served entirely in France and Flanders during the war and fought in every major battle during the battalion's active service, gaining a reliable reputation within a professional, Regular Division and winning many gallantry medals. On February 16th 1918, in line with a major shake up of the British Army, the 8th Battalion was disbanded in France and the men were distributed amongst the other battalions in the regiment.

The battalion was part of the 71st Brigade for their initial period of training in 1915 and for a few weeks in France, but most of their service was within the 16th Brigade, attached to the veteran 6th Division. For the period the 8th battalion served within it, the following battalions formed the 16th Brigade and served together as a tactical unit:

8th Battalion, the Bedfordshire Regiment.
1st Battalion, the Buffs.
1st Battalion, the Kings Shropshire Light Infantry.
2nd Battalion the York and Lancaster Regiment.
In April 1916 the 8th Beds was in the Ypres area of Belgium according to this war diary entry.
15 Apr 1916 – Ijser Canal Bank near Ieper Relieved in Camp "N" by 14th Durham Light Infantry. Entrained at 8pm POPERINGHE and detrain at ASYLUM YPRES and relieved 11th K.R.R. on YSER CANAL BANK between bridges No.2 and 4.

16 Apr 1916 – trenches around Willows near Ieper Relieved 10th Rifle Brigade in left section 16IB Sector. Hd.Qrs & C Coy LA BELLE ALLIANCE A Coy S.18.a., B17, B16 and S16b. B Coy 2 platoon Willows, 2 platoon Willow Walk, D Coy 2 platoon Willows 2 platoon D20 D21.

*17 Apr 1916 In trenches as above – Wounded **Lt.Col.H.C.Jackson [Henry Cholmondeley JACKSON]** & 1 O.R.*

18 Apr 1916 In trenches as above – Killed 1 O.R.

19 Apr 1916 In trenches as above - Wounded 2 O.R. **This is the day Frank was recorded as dying although it is likely to have been 19/20 (see below).**

20 Apr 1916 - Ijser Canal Bank In trenches as above - *Killed - **Capt Quilter, 2Lt Cartwright, 2Lt.McMichael.** *Wounded* **2Lt Vipond, 2Lt Player, 2Lt Charles [William Eugene CHARLES].** *Missing* **2Lt Squier.** *O.Ranks - Killed 32, Missing believed Killed 97, Wounded 65 Relieved by 2/York and Lancaster Regt. - Battalion moved back in support in dugouts on YSER CANAL - *On night 19/20 Apl. after 2 hours heavy bombardment Germans attacked and gained a footing in trenches D20, WILLOW WALK and S18a - D21, B17a and B16 still held by battalion and line VICARS LANE - CLIFFORD TOWER - GANTHORPE ROAD strengthened and reinforced.*

Pte. **Frank Brown's** body was never found/ identified so his name is to be found on the vast Menin Gate Memorial to the Missing in Ypres, Panels 31 and 33. He was 31 years old. According to the newspaper report, his wife waited for nearly a year to have his death confirmed. He was killed instantaneously by a shell. The widow had two small children to care for.

Named on the Menin Gate

Frederick John Brown

Date of Birth: 2-11-1898
First School: Hitchin British Infants' School
Hitchin Boys' British School
Date of Admission: 1-5-1906
Parents: William and Emily
Address on admission: Charlton
Left school: ?   Occupation: ?

1901 Census details

William 34, a yardman (cattle) with his wife Emily 34 were living in Charlton with their children Emily 12, William 11, Charlotte 9, Harry 8, **Frederick 2** and Arthur 6 months.

1911 Census details

Still living in Charlton at Pear Tree Cottage, William 45 was now a horse keeper. Emily 45 had had more children, in fact 16 altogether and only 11 were still alive!

Those at home on the night of the census (April 2nd 1911) were William 21 and Harry 18, farm labourers, **Frederick** 12 was at the British School, Ada 9, Frank 7, Gerald 5, Charles 3, Dorothy 1 and Albert 6 months. They lived in 4 rooms.

Military details

Frederick's service records have in part survived which show that he enlisted for service on October 2nd 1916 in Hitchin at 17 years 11 months. He was examined and 'mobilized' in Bedford on March 24th 1917 and at 5 feet 8 inches and weighing 130lbs. he went into the Training Reserve Battalion (9973). He was transferred to the 6th Middlesex Battalion 9973 then into the 1st Battalion of the Duke of Cambridgeshire's Own (Middlesex Regiment) as G/60128.

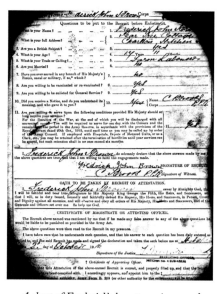

In the first week of January 1918 the Division was moved back into its old sector at Passchendaele. On many occasions the front of the 33rd Division was raided by Germans, particularly from the 'Gasometers' and opposite the railway from the direction of Passchendaele Station.

The 5/6th Scottish Rifles in the 19th Brigade, the 1st M'sex in the 98th Brigade and the 9th Highland Light Infantry in the 100th Brigade took it upon themselves in particular, to keep

A sheet of Frederick's burnt service records

Beautifully tended memorial plots at Tyne Cot

the enemy at a distance and so active were their patrols and so successful, the enemy was seldom to be met within 700 to 1000 yards. Whilst, in front of the left sector, served by the 19th and 98th Brigades, the Gasometers, a point of considerable tactical importance to the enemy, was finally vacated. Except for night bombing and violent 'shell storms' very little activity was shown by the enemy but everyone felt that this was

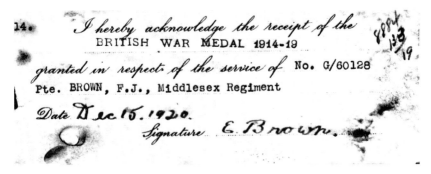

Acknowledgement of receipt of his War Medal signed by his mother

only the lull before the storm. It was, the enemy stormed through on March 29th 1918.

In his time on the Western Front Pte. **Frederick Brown** had seen a great deal and his short life ended during this 'lull' period on March 9th. He has no known grave and he is commemorated on the Tyne Cot Memorial to the Missing, panels 113-115, N.E. of Ypres alongside 35,000 others. He was only 19 years old.

Frederick Cain

Date of Birth: 21-5-1890
First School: Hitchin British Infants' School
Hitchin Boys' British School
Date of Admission: 10-5-1897
Parents: Samuel and Hannah
Address on admission: Union Road [Oughtonhead Way]
Left school: ?   Occupation: Grocer's Boy

1891 Census details

The family was living at 60 Old Park Road. Samuel (born in Lilley), was 33 and a tailor. Hannah aged 33 was a tailoress and was born in Offley. Charles was 9, Percy was 7, Florence H. 5, Winifred V. 5 and **Frederick** 10 months.

1901 Census details

Sadly, Samuel had died aged 37 in 1894 and Hannah died in 1900 aged 42 so the head of the family was now Charles who was 19 and a tailor, Percy 17, was a hairdresser, Florence was 15, Winifred 13 and **Frederick** was 10. They were now living at 4 Kent Place, Union Road.

1911 Census details

Four children were still living together at Kent Place and Percy was living with the Paine family at 56 High Street East Grinstead, Sussex where Mr. Arthur Paine was a hairdresser. Winifred was now a dressmaker and **Frederick,** a grocer's assistant.

Before he enlisted he was working as an assistant at one of the chain of Messrs. Moss the grocers in Baldock.

Military details

None of his service records have survived but from the medal rolls index he was posthumously awarded the 1915 Star as well as the Victory and British War medals so that tells us that he enlisted in 1915 (the press reported February). He went into the 1st Battalion Bedfordshire Regiment, number 19447. He was in the 15th Brigade, 5th Division and by all accounts life was fairly quiet at the beginning of 1916 but then things began to happen as the regimental war diary shows. He was actually named.

War diary June-July 1916

22-26 Jun 1916 Battn. at IZEL-les-HAMEAU. Training in Route marching & open Warfare begun & carried out as far as weather & limited space for training purposes would allow. Weather indifferent - a good deal of rain

27 Jun 1916 - Arras Marched to ARRAS via NOYELLE VION & WANQUETIN about 15 mile, arrived 1 Am (only one man falling out) Good Billets.

28 Jun 1916 In ARRAS. 610 men to find for work under R.A. & 5th Signal Coy R.E. in neighbourhood of WAILLY

29 Jun 1916 780 men working as above [Comment; Sgt 9495 Edwin BARBER DOW]

30 Jun 1916 730 men working as above. 'B' & 'D' Coys moved to WAILLY for work under 5 Signal Coy. R.E. This detachment of 2 Coys. under the command of CAPT. [Frederick Vivian] PARKER

1 Jul 1916 - Arras and Wailly As above. 500 men found for fatigues. B & D Coys at WAILLY, H.Q. & 2 Coys at ARRAS. C.O. & parties of officers reconnoitred neighbourhood of WAILLY & CRINCHON VALLEY.

2 Jul 1916 - Givenchy-le-Noble Ordered suddenly to proceed to GIVENCHY-le-NOBLE 15 m. due W. of ARRAS. Moved out in daylight by sections. Transport followed by night. Good billets. 2 coys in Village. 2 coys & H.Q. in Chateau GIVENCHY-Le-NOBLE 'B' & 'D' Coys heavily shelled in WAILLY before leaving. 4 casualties (wounded) [Comment; Pte 19447 Frederick CAIN died]

He died aged 26 on the second day of the dreadful battle of the Somme having been on the Western Front for about 8 months.

Pte. **Frederick Cain** is buried in the Douchy-Les-Ayette British Cemetery, , plot III, row B, grave 21. When I visited his grave I noted that his family had paid for the inscription 'Not Lost But Gone Before' on his Commonwealth War Graves headstone. Families were invited to have an inscription but they were charged 3 1/2 pence per letter and a maximum of 60 letters was allowed.

The Trio

Wilfred Camfield

Date of Birth: 26-4-1894
First School: Walsworth British School
Hitchin Boys' British School
Date of Admission: 3-6-1901
Parents: Edward (a coachman) and Annie
Address on admission: Tilehouse Street
Left school: 19-5-1904 to go to Knebworth
Occupation: ?

Bedfordshire cap badge

1891 Census details

His father was Edward, born in Knebworth and in 1891 he was a footman at East Dene, Bonchurch, I.O.W. in the household of the County Magistrate. Research suggests that his mother Annie may have died after young **Wilfred's** birth.

1901 Census details

Wilfred 6, was staying with his uncle Frederick Hilsden 36, a horseman on a farm and his wife Lizzie 38 with Cyril B. their 9 year old son. They were living at Grove Farm Cottages, Walsworth. His father, recorded as a widower, was a groom working for Mr Samuel Lucas in Tilehouse Street

1911 Census details

Wilfred was now living with William R. Willcocks 43, a wood merchant and his wife Mary 43, at Winter Green, Codicote. They had no children but **Wilfred** 16 was recorded as their nephew and assisting in the wood business.

In 1915 **Wilfred** married a Miss Stafford.

Research of the Hitchin Boys' British School registers suggest that **Wilfred** had three step-brothers, Ivan, born March 6th 1903, Stanley, born August 28th 1904 and Lionel George, born June 10th 1906. Their mother was Elizabeth A. who married Edward in 1902.

Military details

His service records have not survived but he joined the 8th Bedfordshire Regiment and was awarded the British and Victory medals so one assumes that he joined up around the time of his marriage in 1915. The following entries from the Battalion war diaries show exactly where **Wilfred** was as he moved up from N.E. of Guillemont towards the 'Quadrilateral' with the 8th Beds. It would appear that mistakes were made in the tensions of war and many of the casualties may have been caused by our own fire!

Extracts from the 8th Battalion Bedfordshire War Diary.

13 Sep 1916 - trenches near Guillemont **Capt. Steyne [Pierre STEYNE, DSO]** *with* **B Coy co-operated with 18th Brigade in an attack at 6 am on QUADRILATERAL** *[Ref Longueval T.15.c]. Attack unsuccessful although B Coy bombed their way about 100 yds along German trench causing considerable casualties to the enemy. The attack was repeated at 6 pm with two platoons of C Coy. assisting the 18th Brigade in the frontal attack. Enemy driven in from his advanced posts but QUADRILATERAL not taken.*

14 Sep 1916 Battalion in trenches making all preparations for part in 4th Army offensive on 15th September.

***15 Sep 1916 [Comment: **The Battles of the Somme 1916 - the Battle of Flers-Courcelette]** **Battalion ordered to take QUADRILATERAL** *assisted by the Heavy Section of the M.G. Corps with "TANKS" advance about 500 yds NE. Battn was in a position for attack about 4.30 am ZERO hour 6.20 am Three waves were supplied by D, D [sic] and A Coys under* **Capt Hatch [Robert Bernard Lawson HATCH, MC]**, **2/Lt Hodges [Archibald Gordon HODGES]** *and* **Lt Draisey [Edwin Roland Watts DRAISEY]** *respectively to attack the QUADRILATERAL, which was on our left flank, whilst B Coy co-operated by bombing down the trench leading to it. At 6.0 am heavy artillery opened a slow barrage on Line MORVAL - LES BOEUFS. At ZERO hour (6.20 am) intense artillery barrage opened and unluckily was cut short where our 3 companies were drawn up for the attack in shell holes. This mistake caused many casualties. Our attacking companies pushed forward and though supported by 1/The Buffs and later re-enforced by the 2/York & Lancaster Regt failed to take the position. "TANKS" did not arrive to assist and the position was not heavily shelled previous to the attack. Brigade ordered original*

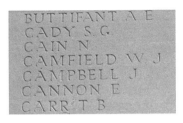

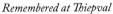
Remembered at Thiepval

Thiepval Memorial to the Missing

trenches to be held and await orders. As battalion had suffered very severely in casualties, 6 Officers killed and 7 wounded, we were relieved by 2/Y & L at 6.0 pm and put in brigade reserve in trenches S.E. of GUILLEMONT.

Pte. **Wilfred Camfield** was killed on September 15th and his body was not found so he is commemorated on the Thiepval Memorial to the Missing alongside 74,000 others, Pier and Face 2C. He was just 22.

·—·• • **● ● ●** • •—·

Lionel Norman Day

Date of Birth: 9-8-1895
First School: St Saviour's Infant
Hitchin Boys' British School
Date of Admission: 1-5-1903
Parents: Richard N. (market gardener) and Amy Laura
Address on admission: 95 Walsworth Road
Left school: 29-7-1909   Occupation: Greengrocer

1901 Census details

Richard Norman 32, a market gardener and his wife Amy Laura 30, were living at 95 Walsworth Road. with their children **Lionel Norman 5**, Gerald Stanley 3, Elsie 1 and Eleanor Asman 18, a servant. The greengrocery/fruiterers business was run from the shop there.

1911 Census details

Richard was now recorded as a Fruiterer and market gardener and had been married to Amy for 17 years. **Lionel,** now 15, was an assistant market gardener working in his father's business, Gerald was 13 and more children had been born; Gordon Fred 5, Robert Steven 3 and Annette Theresa 1. Elsie was living with her grandmother Stevens at 138 Nightingale Road. One of their children

Lionel Day's family 1915

had died but 6 were living. Two more children followed, Philip Arthur, the father of my family contact member Mrs Susan Hamilton, and one other, Eric.

Before joining the army **Lionel** assisted his father in his business as a greengrocer and fruiterer at Walsworth Road. He was a member of the Church Lads' Brigade and the Blue Cross Brigade.

Military details

We know that Lionel joined up on April 8th 1916 and became Private 34906 in the 8th Battalion, Royal Fusiliers, City of London Regiment, 36th Brigade, 12th (Eastern) Division. After initial basic training he went over to France on July 4th, just 4 days into the big push at the Battle of the Somme. He was sadly wounded 3 weeks later and was captured. Because his service records have not survived, we do not know whether he had been catapulted into action so soon or whether he was on his way to the front.

Certainly on July 7th the 8th Battalion was in action trying to get a foothold in Ovillers, N.E. of Albert. They did but were not able to hold their gains and were forced back with heavy casualties recorded (640). They were then relieved and went back behind the lines to Albert (July 9th), Senlis ((July 10th), Forceville ((July 11th), Bus-Les-Artois ((July 12th) and Mailly-Maillet ((July

His Memorial Card

20th), trenches north of Auchonvillers and Bois de Warnimont (25/7). This it would seem was when he was captured, wounded and taken to a prisoner of war camp at Wissen in Germany. He recovered from the wounds but contracted pneumonia and sadly died exactly a year after going to France, on July 4th 1917 aged 21.

The newspaper report states that Pte. **Lionel Day** was laid to rest with British tradition, a wreath of roses being placed on his grave.

According to information from his niece Mrs Susan Hamilton of Fareham, Hampshire, he was first buried in Wissen then was re-interred in the Cologne Southern Cemetery, plot V, row H, grave 10.

The medal roll index shows that his family would have received the British and Victory medals as well as the 'Dead Man's Penny' which every family received after the death of their soldier.

Interestingly his brother Gerald Stanley joined up in the 54th Division, Signal Company R.E. as 528068 on January 19th 1915 in Bury St Edmunds. His service records have survived and it appears that he qualified as a 'Field Linesman' in what was part of the Egyptian Expeditionary Force on October 1st 1918. He was admitted to hospital there twice with malaria and was finally 'de-mobbed' on June 14th 1919 in Alexandria. His return to the family business in Walsworth Road must have been a happy occasion tinged with much sadness, in that they had lost their firstborn.

Lionel's grave

William Maynard Dimmock

Date of Birth: 5-1-1876
First School: ?
Hitchin Boys' British School
Date of Admission: 13-12-1886
Parents: William and Sarah
Address on admission: ?
Left school: 6-2-1887   Occupation: ?

Essex Regiment cap badge

1881 Census details

Father William 34, a photographic artist, (born in Bermondsey) and Sarah his wife 34 (born Great Hadham, Herts), were living at 29 ½ Little Thomas Street Lambeth with their children Rosa 6, **William Maynard** 4 (born Codicote), Esther Elizabeth 3, and Henry John 1.

1891 Census details

The family was now living at 4 Wratten Road. Rosa was now a general servant, **William Maynard** 15, was a photographer's assistant, Henry was now 11 and in addition Rebecca M 8, Emily 6, Arthur 4 and Walter 1 had been born.

1901 Census details

William Maynard was now 25, a bricklayer's labourer and married to Julia (née Moles). They were living with her widowed mother Fanny Moles 60, at Osier Bed Cottage, St Ippolyts with William's brother Henry 21, a photographer's assistant and 3 others.

1911 Census details

William Maynard was now 35 and a general labourer and had been married for 10 years to Julia. They had 3 daughters, Fanny Elizabeth 10, Maud Millicent 5 and Minnie, 1 and were living at 3 Black Horse Lane in 4 rooms. **William** demonstrated good handwriting; a credit to his schooling!

Military details

William enlisted in Ampthill in 1915 and went over to France in 1916. He was first 22704 in the 8th Bedfordshire Regiment then he was due to be transferred into the reserve list of the 17th Essex Regiment but was deemed unfit in January 1917. Much detective work was needed for this soldier!

The 17th Essex - On January 1st 1917 the 67th Provisional Battalion was at Sheringham in the 223rd Brigade which became the 17th Battalion (Essex). It had been formed in 1915 from Home Service personnel of Territorial

Force Battalions. By July 1917 it was at Weybourne in 223rd Brigade where it remained. So the 17th Essex never went abroad and it has to be assumed that he was injured whilst serving with the Bedfordshire Regiment. Pension records show this to be so. He had gun shot wounds to the right hip on May 22nd 1916 (near Ypres, Belgium) which at his medical in January 1917 it was said, needed the use of a walking stick. The 8th Beds were at that date in trenches near the Yser Canal, north of Ypres.

Pte. **William Dimmock** sadly died on April 27th 1917 aged 41 back in England and is buried in the Hitchin Cemetery, N.E. Extension, grave 515 with the family's inscription, 'Nearer my God to Thee'.

John Farr

Date of Birth: 13-10-1890
First School: Hitchin British Infants' School
Hitchin Boys' British School
Date of Admission: 9-5-1898
Parents: John and Ada
Address on admission: 99 Queen Street
(grandmother dealt with his admission)
Left school: ?
Occupation: ?

John Farr's birthplace in Buntingford

This family gave me an incredible amount of head-scratching but after time-consuming research and with dogged determination I concluded their story.

1881 Census details

Living at the Globe Inn at 79 High Street, Buntingford, John (snr.) a beer house keeper 28, had married Hannah (née Hills) aged now 31 on 29.12.1879 and had taken on her son Woodley Cody (sic) aged 9. They had 7 lodgers including a fishmonger, a tailor and his wife and 4 musicians, 3 of them being German.

1891 Census details

Hannah died in 1888 but had Lizzie in 1882 and Alfred in 1884.

By now John had re-married an Ada and they had **John** aged 1. They also had 2 lodgers staying at the Globe Inn with them. Sadly his second wife, Ada died in 1895, aged 30. It would seem now that John took his young children to live with his parents James and Eliza Farr in Hitchin, his birthplace.

1901 Census details

The grandparents were living at 11 Biggin Lane. James 72, (born in Preston, Herts.), was a general dealer and his wife Eliza (née Maylin) 71, had been born in Hitchin. Living with them were Harry 17, Alfred 15 and **John** 10 years old. Alfred and **John** were their grandchildren and were born in Buntingford where their father was the licensee of the Globe Public House. I cannot account for Harry.

I can find no details of John (snr) in 1901 and by the time of the 1911 census he was living alone in Ware and he was a fishmonger, but later that year, on Christmas Day he married again, an Elizabeth Bateman (32). They were living at 119 Turner Row, Bow, London and he was recorded as a 56 year old widower and fishmonger on the marriage certificate. Sadly he died in 1915 in Ware.

1911 Census details

Our **John** (20), was lodging with the Maylin family at 4 Gascoine's Yard, Queen Street He was a marine dealer, self employed and working from home.

From the newspaper article in 1917 it transpired that Elizabeth (Lizzie), his sister had married Herbert Maylin. Herbert, 28 was a signal painter with the G.N. Railway, Elizabeth was 29 and they had Walter 7, Leonard 5 and Phyllis, 7 months.

Military details

John Farr enlisted in Bedford in April 1916 and after training went abroad on Boxing Day 1916. He was formerly 6347 in the Essex Regiment but transferred into the Bedfordshire Regiment (33860).

In the early part of 1917 **John's** battalion was in the area of Loos/Hulluch. There was much trench work, drilling, musketry training and equipment cleaning as well as games of football and teams of Tug-of-War. The weather in April made the conditions in the trenches very difficult and the Battalion war diary describes in detail on a daily basis exactly what the troops were enduring. There were some quiet days with little enemy activity then there would be dreadful machine gun attacks and much enemy aircraft activity.

We know from the newspaper report on September 22nd 1917 that **John** was wounded during this period but as his service records have not survived we cannot know the full details.

The battalion in September were in trenches on Hill 70 preparing for a big attack on the 13th. in order to oust the Germans from Bois Hugo (Hugo Wood). **John** was killed by a shell which brushed close to him and one other, in either Huxley, Hythe or Hurdle trench on Hill 70. Pte. **John Farr** was buried in St Patrick's Cemetery, Loos, plot 2, row D, grave 15 aged just 26.

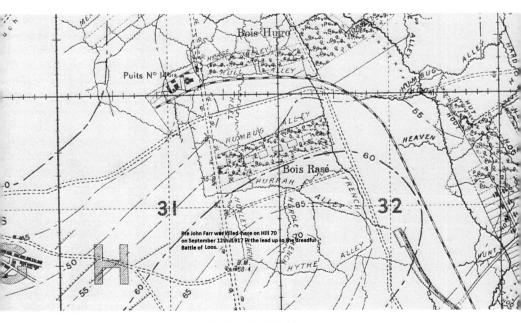

The Loos Battlefield

George William Alfred Farrow

Date of Birth: 6-3-1898
First School: Hitchin British Infants' School
Hitchin Boys' British School
Date of Admission: 2-5-1904
Parents: Alfred George and Marie
Address on admission: Duckland's Farm
Left school: 19-6-1911
Occupation: Errand boy

George Farrow's
Memorial plaque

1901 Census details

The family was living at Duckland's Farm with grandparents George F. 71, an agricultural labourer and Betsy (née Cooper) 67. Alfred George 23 (born Shillington), a horsekeeper and Marie 23, née Marie Therese Oppenheim, the daughter of a watchmaker from Hamburg lived with them. (She was born in London). Their son **George William Alfred** 3, was born in Kentish Town.

1911 Census details

Alfred and Marie both 32 were still living at Duckland's Farm and **George** was now 13, Dorothy 4, Reginald 1 and Margaret 6 months, had been born.

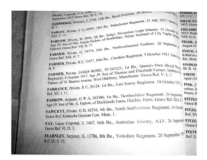

The Book of Remembrance at the
Hooge Crater Cemetery

Hooge Crater Cemetery

Military details

George Farrow joined the Herts. Territorials in January 1914 and was at camp with them when war broke out. The newspaper report says that he joined up with his school friend James Sewell. No service or pension records have survived but we know that he had no. 2313 in the Bedfordshire Regiment from the medal card details but when he was killed, he is recorded as Sergeant 265385 1st Battalion Hertfordshire Regiment. From his medals entitlement we know that he went overseas on November 6th 1914 as he was awarded the 1914 Star as well as the War and Victory medals.

The 1st Battalion Hertfordshire Regiment was part of the 118th Brigade, 39th Division.

In **1914** the battalion was lightly involved in The Battles of Ypres 1914 (also called The First Battle of Ypres).

In **1915** the battalion was engaged during the winter actions at Cuinchy in February, the Battle of Festubert in May and at the Battle of Loos in September.

In **1916** the battalion was engaged in the Battles of the Somme, including being lightly involved in the Battle of the Ancre Heights in October, as well as in the Battle of the Ancre in November.

In **1917** the battalion was heavily engaged during the opening day of the Battles of Ypres 1917 (also called the Third Battle of Ypres and Passchendaele) when the battalion lost over 450 men during their assault on St Julien, part of the Battle of Pilkem. They were also involved less heavily in the Battle of Langemarck in August, the Battle of the Menin Road and the Battle of Polygon Wood in September.

From the newspaper report we know that he had been home on leave twice, gassed once and wounded once.

The Battle of Polygon Wood was the action when our soldier **Sgt. Farrow** was killed on September 26th 1917 at the tender age of 19 years 6 months. He had seen so much action in his short life. He is buried at Hooge Crater Cemetery, plot IXA, row D, grave 2. The family still has his Memorial Plaque, kindly loaned by Keith Monk and Angela Hillyard. (see photo).

Gerald Henry Field

Date of Birth: 7-3-1895
First School: St Saviour's
Hitchin Boys' British School
Date of Admission: 1-5-1902
Parents: Henry (railway shunter) and Mary A
Address on admission: 29 Ickleford Road
Left school: 17-3-1910   Occupation: ?

1901 Census details

Father, Henry 32, who was born in Gosmore was a 'Goods Guard' and mother Mary 30,who was born in Ley Green, Kings Walden only had **Gerald** 6, (born at Well Head). The family was living at 29, Ickleford Road.

1911 Census details

The family was still at the same address and young **Gerald**, 16 was an apprentice engine fitter.

Military details

It would appear from the obituary that was in the local newspaper on May 11th 1916 that Mr Field Snr. a caretaker at the Town Hall, had lost his wife and now suffered the loss of his only son at 21 years. Stoker 1st Class **Gerald Field** (K 20039) had been in the navy for 3 years and was part of the crew of HMS "Ettrick", a torpedo boat destroyer. "He, like thousands of other brave fellows has had a strenuous time in searching the seas for enemy craft. He caught a cold which brought on a fatal illness" (*Herts Express*).

C.W.G. Certificate

Gerald Field's ship, HMS Ettrick

His death occurred at Haslar Hospital, Gosport on May 10th 1916 when in fact he was attached to HMS "Pembroke" which was a shore establishment at Chatham. A service was held at Hitchin Parish Church where he had been a choir boy and interment followed at the Hitchin cemetery (S.E.915). His father would have received the 1914 Star and the War and Victory medals after his son's death.

George Foster (brother of Harry)

Date of Birth: 3-5-1885
First School: St Mary's Infant School
Hitchin Boys' British School
Date of Admission: 19-9-1892
Parents: George and Phoebe
Address on admission: Charlton
Left school: 7-2-1896   Occupation: ?

1891 Census details

Father George (born Gosmore), was 28 but recorded as 31 and a farm labourer. His wife Phoebe (born on Alderney in the Channel Islands) was 24. They were living in Charlton and had Albert 8, **George 7,** Charles 5 and Harry 8 months.

1891 census for George Foster

1901 Census details

(Henry) George Foster was 38 and Phoebe 34. They had the following children with them in Charlton, **George 16** (Ag. Lab. working for Mr W. Anderson), Charles 15, Harry 10, Sidney 7, Leonard 5, John 3 and Richard 1.

1911 Census details

The family was now living at 52 Queen Street with 7 children still living at home. Phoebe had had 11 children and had lost 4. **George, 26,** was a farm labourer as was Harry.

Military Details

George joined the East Surrey Regiment with the number 2644 and went over to France on October 5th 1915 so his medal's card shows the 1914-15 Star and the War and Victory medals. We know from the newspaper report that he was wounded 4 times and on leaving hospital the last time he wrote home. The poor man had really suffered in his long war. But then on April 9th 1918 a letter was written from the regimental chaplain on his behalf. "Because my left arm is severely wounded and I shall not be able to write for a long time. I'm going into hospital again."

The next letter home from the chaplain said that **George** died the next day on April 10th in the casualty clearing station. This was either the 33rd or the 54th casualty clearing station as these were the two which used this small cemetery between April and August 1918. The regiment was at Grenas at the time and the war diary doesn't indicate action at that time, it says that the men were cleaning up the billets after rain so presumably it was a stray shell or similar. Private **George Foster** was buried at Haverskerque British Cemetery, north of Béthune with a grave reference B2. He was 32 years old although the C.W.G.C. certificate indicates 37. This was a second blow for the family who were now living at 8 Fairview Cottages, Kershaw's Hill, as Harry had been killed in 1916.

Harry Foster (brother of George)

Date of Birth: July 1890
First School: Hitchin British Infants' School
Hitchin Boys' British School
Date of Admission: 31-10-1898
Parents: George (agricultural labourer) and Phoebe
Address on admission: Charlton
Left school: 1-7-1904
Occupation: Farm Boy

The War and Victory medals

Census details *(see above)*

Military details

Research uncovered the fact that **Harry** married Alice Louisa Sole (from Kelshall, nr. Royston) on December 21st 1913 in St Mary's Parish Church and resided at 8 Fairview Cottages, Kershaw's Hill. From the medal rolls index it appears he went over to Belgium after the beginning of 1916 as he was awarded the War and Victory medals. His wife produced John who was born and died in 1914 and Harry Charles William (1916-1969).

Harry Foster's service records have not survived but we know that he was Private 18314 in the 8th Battalion Bedfordshire Regiment. It would seem that he died shortly after arriving at the front in the Ypres area of Belgium. From the war diary it seems that his battalion was heavily shelled on February 12th 1916 and as he died on the 13th, he would have died of wounds as there didn't seem to be any real action on 13th. Casualties suffered from smoke and gas in this bombardment.

He is buried nearby in La Brique Military Cemetery 2, plot 1, row S, grave 25. He was 25. Today, the cemetery is surrounded by houses. When I visited his grave with a remembrance poppy, on a sunny December morning, I found the family's inscription 'Peace Perfect Peace' at the base of his headstone. One wonders whether Alice or the family was ever able to visit?

Cemetery entrance

Bertram William Froy

Date of Birth: 6-8-1888
First School: Hitchin British Infants' School
Hitchin Boys' British School
Date of Admission: 10-6-1895
Parents: William and Sarah
Address on admission: 96 Queen Street
Left school: 26-9-1902   Occupation: Draper's errand boy

1891 Census details

The family was living at 96 Queen Street. William was 42 and a house painter, his wife Sarah was 44. They had Alfred 18, Frank 15, Arthur 8, Lizzie 6 and Leonard 8 months. **Bertram** at 2 ½ was not at home and had probably been farmed out to relatives but I cannot find him.

1901 Census details

Still at 96 Queen Street William at 51 was a widower. Sarah had died in 1898. The following children were living at home, Alfred 27, Emma 22, (she was not on the 1891 census) Arthur 18, Lizzie 15 and **Bertram** 12. All the children were born in Hitchin.

1911 Census details

Bertram married Elizabeth Jane Kerbyshire in early 1909 and in the 1911 census they were living at 2 Biggin Lane. Bertram was now 22 and his wife 23 and they had little Annie E. aged 2. He was a bricklayer.

Military details

He enlisted in Bedford in November 1915 and the medal index shows his widow would have received the War and Victory medal so we know that he went over to the battlefields after the beginning of 1916, the war diary suggests July 25th 1916. He was Pte.30592 in the 4th Battalion Bedfordshire Regiment.

Pte. **Bertram Froy** was killed on February 11th 1917 aged 28 in the River Ancre sector (Somme) and his name appears on the Thiepval Memorial, Pier 2c. as his body was not found/identified. It was not until September of that year that his wife received official confirmation at her home, 3 Seymour's Yard and the very next day she was summoned to Arlesey where her mother had suddenly died whilst cooking a meal for an injured Canadian soldier! This was a double blow for the poor mother of two children, the eldest being 8. The widow seems to have soon remarried as she appears as Mrs Hulbert (formerly Froy) and living at 51 Lonsdale Road, Bayswater London when the War Graves Commission registered his death on the certificate.

Bertram's name in need of renovation

Ernest Arnold Grant (brother of Leonard)

Date of Birth: 25-9-1895
First School: Hitchin British Infants' School
Hitchin Boys' British School
Date of Admission: 1-5-1903
Parents: Frederick (a house painter) and Amelia
Address on admission: 7 Trevor Road
Left school: 24-9-1909   Occupation: Bootseller

1901 Census details

The family was living at 2 Nursery Villas, Queen Street and consisted of Frederick 34, a house painter, Amelia 35, Bertram 9, Leonard P. 7, **Ernest A.** 5 and Walter 3. They were all born in Hitchin.

1911 Census details

They were now living at 'Hazeldene', Storehouse Lane in 6 rooms. Frederick 44, was still a house painter, Amelia was 45, Bertram F. was now 19 and working as a painter, **Ernest** 15, was a boot seller at Freeman Hardy Willis, Walter was 13 and Doris L. had been born. Leonard was living elsewhere.

Military details

Ernest enlisted (with his older brother Bertram F) in Chelsea as 4600 3/1st County of London Yeomanry, then he was G/62200 in the 4th Battalion, Royal Fusiliers (City of London Regiment). This was in the 3rd Division, 9th Brigade. From the war medal rolls we know he would have been in service after the beginning of 1916 but, unlike his other brother Leonard, none of his records remain.

By March 1917 the allies had started to push the enemy back from the Somme during their retreat behind the Hindenburg Line. The 3rd Division would have been involved in that prior to going up to Arras for the start

of the Battle of Arras (the first Battle of the Scarpe) on April 9th 1917. Pte. **Ernest Grant** is buried in the Faubourg D'Amiens Cemetery, Arras plot II, row J, grave 7 and was killed by a shell on March 21st according to his serving brother Bertram. He was buried the next day. On his headstone is the family's inscription at the base, 'Thy Will Be Done'. He was just 21.

Faubourg D'Amiens Cemetery, Arras

Leonard Grant (brother of Ernest)

Date of Birth: 27-10-1893
First School: Hitchin British Infants' School
Hitchin Boys' British School
Date of Admission: 21-5-1900
Parents: Frederick (a house painter) and Amelia
Address on admission: Queen Street
Left school: 25-10-1907   Occupation: House painter

Royal Engineers cap badge

The census details are the same as for his brother Ernest.

In 1911 **Leonard** was lodging with his uncle William Arnold and family at Parkstone, Dorset and was working as a grocer's assistant.

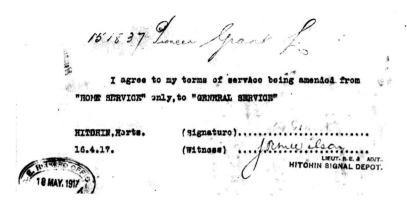

Having signed up for home service, he agreed to war service

Military details

He enlisted on January 14th 1916 (in Hitchin) in the Royal Engineers as Sapper 151837, giving his address as 51 Queen Street. Some of his service records remain, so we have his personal profile and know that he was 22 years 2 months old, 6 feet tall and weighed 130 lbs. He was working as a grocer. He seems to have no medal entitlement and no mention of going overseas on his Service Record. He was mobilised June 14th 1917. He agreed to go abroad but seemingly did not do so. Having passed his Trade Test he appears to have been kept in the U.K. as a Royal Engineer before going into hospital on October 31st 1918 with influenza and pneumonia. He got progressively worse

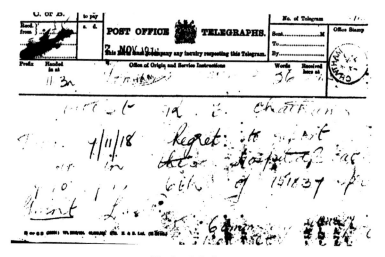

The dreaded telegram

according to the records and died on November 6th 1918 at 8.20pm in the Barnet War Hospital aged 25. This was just 4 days after the death of his mother who had also succumbed to the same dreadful illness. Sadly he had married during his time in service, a lady called Ethel May St John on July 27th 1917 who was living at 51 Queen Street (possibly the home of her in-laws) when she was given the 13/4d per week pension after his death.

Sapper Leonard Grant is buried in Hitchin Cemetery S. VIII B.

Horace James Green (brother of John Henry)

Date of Birth: 9-11-1896
First School: Hitchin British Infants' School
Hitchin Boys' British School
Date of Admission: 12-1-1904
Parents: Arthur (a French polisher) and Maria
Address on admission: 109 Whinbush Road
Left school: 28-10-1910
Occupation: Outfitter's boy

1901 Census details

With the address being 27 Wratten Road, the family consisted of Arthur 50, a French polisher (born Brixton) Maria 40, (born Manchester) Alice 16, William 14, a leather cutter's assistant, Florence 12, Edward 10, Lilian 9, (all born in London) John 6, **Horace 4,** (both born St Ippolyts) Christopher 2 and Albert 3 months, (both born in Hitchin)..

Hertfordshire cap badge

1911 Census details

They were now living at 109 Whinbush Road in a 7 roomed house. Arthur at 60 was a French polisher dealing in antiques. His wife Maria to whom he had been married for 29 years was 50 and was now a boarding house keeper as they had 4 boarders. Their 12 children were all surviving but some had left home, John included. I suspect he joined the army because he certainly was a regular soldier in 1914 though I can't find him listed on the 1911 census.

Lillian Edith was 19, **Horace James 14,** Albert Victor 10, Philip Nuttall 8 and Stanley Nuttall 6, were all at home. The boarders were William George Campbell 29, a musician, his wife Edith 26, an actress and their child Agnes 3, also Emma Mortimer 58 was there as a housekeeper.

Military details

Horace enlisted in Hertford as he was in the Territorials at the outset of war. He had two medals and both a Bedfordshire Regimental number (265939) and a Hertfordshire Regimental number (3295) the latter being his number upon death. Many men who lived in Hertfordshire enlisted in the Bedfordshire Regiment. The Herts and Beds.Regiments amalgamated in 1918 after his death.

Following are the details from the 1st Battalion Herts war diary when it was in the area Givenchy-Cuinchy.

19-7-16. A party of about 3 Officers and 60 OR's raided the enemy's trenches at 10.40pm. The part of the trench that was raided had been evacuated by the Germans. The party was in the trenches for 10 minutes as arranged but was bombed from the support line. No prisoners were taken. Our casualties on the evening of the raid were 3 Officers wounded, 3 OR's killed, 1 OR missing, 12 OR's wounded.

24-7-16. The Battalion were relieved by the 12th Royal Sussex and marched to billets near GORRE having had 16 days in the trenches. Casualties for this period; 1 Officer (Lieut. Veere Smith [John Veere SMITH]) died of wounds, 7 Officers wounded (Captain W.L. Grice [William Lucas GRICE], Lieut. L.G. Gold [Leslie G. GOLD, MC & Bar] (slight), Captain C.F. Hacker [Charles Frederick HACKER, MC, RAMC] (at duty), 2/Lieut. J.W. Smith [John W. SMITH], Lieut. R.P. Loyd [Reginald Percy LOYD], 2/Lieut. W.F. Francis [Wilfred Frederick FRANCIS, MC], Captain B.C. Molony [Brian Charles MOLONY]). 11 OR killed, 1 OR missing, 38 OR's wounded including two Company Sgt. Majors.

26-7-16. The Battalion were marched to L'ECOLE DE JEUNE FILLES, BETHUNE.

Pte. **Horace Green** was killed on July 23rd 1916 aged 19, no doubt whilst still in the trenches after the raid of 19th and waiting to be relieved. He is remembered on the Loos Memorial to the Missing, Panel 135. His parents did not receive official confirmation of his death until December 1917 and according to a newspaper report they had then lost 2 sons and had 3 more still serving. Edward Charles was with the Canadian Foresters (France), Christopher Howard was with the Royal Flying Corps in Norfolk and William was a petty officer in the navy and had seen action with the sinking of the 'Dresden' just before he went home on leave at which point his ship was sunk! (report Dec. 1st 1917)

Loos Memorial and cemetery

53

John Henry Green (brother of Horace)

Date of Birth: 15-11-1894
First School: Hitchin British Infants' School
Hitchin Boys' British School
Date of Admission: 1-5-1901
Parents: Arthur and Maria
Address on admission: 27 Wratten Road
Left school: 13-11-1908
Occupation: Shop assistant

3rd Dragoon Guard's cap badge

The census details are the same as for his brother Horace.

Military details

From his medal's entitlement card we know that **John** went over to the front on October 31st 1914 confirming that he was already a regular soldier at the outbreak of war. In fact he had joined up in 1909. He was number 5392 in the 3rd Dragoon Guards (Prince of Wales' Own) Regiment.

This unit was in Egypt in August and left Alexandria for Liverpool on September 29th, arriving on October 18th. They left for France on 31st and on November 4th were put into the 6th Brigade, (3rd. Division). On this day a great drama was unfolding east of Ypres on the Menin Road where the enemy were on the point of breaking through the line but the gallant 2nd Worcesters and South Wales Borderers held it in the famous stand at Geluveld.

The 6th Cavalry Brigade was rushed up to Sanctuary Wood which is about 3 miles west of Geluveld and put in reserve. Poor 19 year old Private **John Green** had only been in Belgium for less than a week when he was killed in action 6 days later on November 6th. There was much fighting over this ground and his body was not recovered so he is commemorated on Panel 3 of the Menin Gate Memorial to the Missing alongside many of our boys.

A visit there on a sunny December morning gave me easy access to the panel which was the first one on the huge Menin Gate approached from the town side. His name was soon found, though with a zoom lens, right at the top. He will be remembered.

Menin Gate Panel

Edward Christopher Halsey

Date of Birth: 12-11-1898
First School: St Saviour's Infant
Hitchin Boys' British School
Date of Admission: 8-5-1905
Parents: John Edward (a butcher) and Minnie A.
Address on admission: 106 Nightingale Road
Left school: 13-2-1914   Occupation: Grocer

1901 Census details.

The family was living at 106 Nightingale Road. John 35, (born in Tewin) was a butcher's assistant, His wife Minnie A. (born in Crowland, Lincs.) was 38. Their children were John T. 6, Joseph 4, Mary 3 and **Edward C.** 2 who were all born in Welwyn.

1911 Census details

The family was now living at 31 Grove Road. Full names were recorded in this census so we know that John Edward at 45 was still a butcher's assistant. His wife Minnie Augusta was 48 and their children were John Titus 16, a 'learner' at the Post Office, Joseph, 14 was a baker's assistant, Mary Jane 13 and **Edward Christopher** 12 were at school. The parents had been married for 17 years and were living in 5 rooms.

The grocery business of George Halsey was set up in 1852 in the Market Place with evidence in the censuses. In 1881 it says that he was employing 4 men and 3 boys. Could he have been employing John Edward in subsequent years?

When **Edward** left school he worked at Latchmore's grocery establishment at 26 High Street before joining up just 3 years later in 1917.

Military details

Edward enlisted in Hitchin in February 1917 and became G/25405 in the 3rd/4th Battalion, Queen's (Royal West Surrey) Regiment. He would have been in training for some time and after reaching his 19th birthday in November 1917 he left England.

The battalion became attached to 62nd Brigade, 21st Division in August 1917 and were involved in the Battles of Ypres (Sept-Nov.) and the Battle of Cambrai (Dec.)

Access to the war diaries for January 12th 1918 shows that his battalion was relieving the 1st Lincoln Regiment in trenches around Vaucelette Farm east of Heudicourt for 4 days until the 16th.

The relief took two hours from 4.30 to 6.30pm. 'Hostile artillery was spasmodically active around the battalion H.Q. during the evening. Trenches in very wet condition. Casualties, other ranks, 1 killed, 4 wounded.'

Edward was the soldier who was killed on that day. Further research in the *Herts Express* newspaper of January 26th 1918, revealed that indeed he was killed instantly by a shell exploding near him and his commanding officer and chaplain both wrote to his parents explaining the circumstances and extending their condolences. He was 19.

Pte. **Edward Halsey** is buried in Fins New British Cemetery, Sorel-Le-Grand, plot III, row F, grave 28. His family had paid for the inscription, 'We Shall Meet Again' and when I visited on a bright May day, the theme in the beautiful planting scheme was a lovely lilac colour.

HITCHIN LAD'S SACRIFICE.

PRIVATE E. C. HALSEY KILLED.

Mr. and Mrs. J. Halsey, 31, Grove-road, Hitchin, have received the sad news of the death in France on January 12 of their youngest son, Private Edward Christopher Halsey, Queen's Royal West Surrey Regiment.

Private Halsey is one of those who, before leaving their teens, have given their lives for England, for he only reached his nineteenth birthday in November last, when he left England for service abroad. Before joining up in February of last year he had worked in Latchmore's grocery establishment, High-street, for some three years.

Private Halsey's parents have received a letter from their son's commanding officer stating that although he had only been a short time with the regiment, he had already shown himself to be a youth of fine type and character, and his death was a great loss to the regiment, as well as to his family. It might be a comfort to his parents to know that he suffered no pain (a shell bursting near, killing him instantly), and that he died doing his duty.

The chaplain writes:—" He was always a regular attendant at my services, and I knew him as a good-hearted lad."

Heartfelt sympathy will be extended to Mr. and Mrs. Halsey in their bereavement. They have two older sons serving with the Colours, Sapper John T. W. Halsey, Royal Engineers, who has been in Salonica for the past two years, and Private Joseph Halsey, who is in France in the Machine Gun Corps.

LETTER FROM AN ARLESEY PRISONER.

Mr. and Mrs. W. Bowskill, of Arlesey, have received the following letter, dated

Fins Cemetery

William Charles Harper

Date of birth: 7-5-1894
First School: Melbourn British School
Hitchin Boys' British School
Date of Admission: 22-11-1904
Parents: Charles and Louisa
Address on admission: 48 Whinbush Road
Left school: ?   Occupation: Gardener

1914 Star Trio

1891 Census details

Reuben Charles Harper (born Melbourn, Cambs.) was 17, the son of James and Elizabeth and they were living at Moor End, Melbourn Cambridgeshire. He was to be the father of our pupil William.

1901 Census details

Reuben, who called himself Charles was married in 1894/5 to Louisa (born Woolmer Green) and in 1901 they were living at The Moor, Melbourn and had two children, **William Charles, 6** and Henry John 4. They were living in Whinbush Road at number 48 by 1904 when William was admitted to our school.

1911 Census details

The census shows father Reuben Charles 36, as a labourer for the Urban District Council and his wife Louisa was 34. Sixteen year old **William** was a gardener and his brother Henry John was 14 and they had a boarder living in. The couple declared they had been married for 17 years and they were living at 95 Whinbush Road, in 5 rooms.

Military details

William, being already in the Territorials, enlisted as 265438 in Hitchin in the 1st Battalion Hertfordshire Regiment. Sadly no service or pension records have survived but he was awarded 3 medals showing his involvement as early as November 6th 1914 for that is when his battalion landed in France.

He received a bullet wound in the head in March 1915 and after a short stay in hospital in Rouen, returned to duty. He came home to Hitchin on leave for Christmas 1916, returning to the front on January 7th 1917.

The 1st/1st battalion served entirely on the Western Front throughout the war and was engaged in the following battles:

*In **1914** they were lightly involved in The Battles of Ypres 1914 (also called The First Battle of Ypres).*

In **1915** *the battalion was engaged during the Winter actions at Cuinchy in February, the Battle of Festubert in May and at the Battle of Loos in September.*

In **1916** *the battalion was engaged in the Battles of the Somme 1916, including being lightly involved in the Battle of the Ancre Heights in October, as well as in the Battle of the Ancre in November.*

In **1917** *the battalion was heavily engaged during the opening day of the Battles of Ypres 1917 (also called the Third Battle of Ypres and Passchendaele), when the battalion lost over 450 men during their assault on St Julien, part of the Battle of Pilkem. They were also involved less heavily in the Battle of Langemarck in August, the Battle of the Menin Road and the Battle of Polygon Wood in September, as well as the Second Battle of Passchendaele in October.*

During **1918**, *the battalion was again heavily engaged. During the First Battles of the Somme 1918 (also called the German Spring Offensives, Operation Michael and Kaiserschlacht), they were heavily involved in the Battle of St Quentin, the actions on the Somme crossings and the Battle of Rosieres in March. In April they were also engaged in the Battle of the Lys, namely the First and Second Battles of Kemmel as well as the Battle of Scherpenberg, during which time their already exhausted Division fought as Composite Battalions.*

WAR NEWS

TERRITORIAL SERGEANT,

HITCHIN LOSES SOLDIER WHO
FOUGHT FROM 1914.

The distressing news that her eldest son, Sergeant W. C. Harper, Herts. Regiment, has died of wounds received in action in France has been received by Mrs. Harper, 17, Grove-road, Hitchin. Sergeant Harper was seriously wounded in the head on March 25, and died in the 6th General Hospital, Rouen, on April 11.

Writing to Mrs. Harper, the Chaplain of the Hospital says: — "Your son was not in a state to leave any . messages He will be buried in a cemetery near by, with full military honours. God bless and comfort you, and be proud of a brave son, who gave his life for others."

The Sister of the Hospital writes :—" Your son was going on fairly well, but got worse last evening and died early this morning. He had a very bad wound in the head, and I am afraid there was little chance of his recovering properly."

Sergeant Harper was a member of the Herts. Territorials, and went to France with them on November 5, 1914. He was wounded in the head by a bullet in March, 1915, and after a short stay in hospital at Rouen, returned to duty. He came home on leave on December 24, 1916, and returned to France on January 7, 1917. He was a member of the Hitchin Blue Cross Club, and prior to mobilisation was a gardener at the Benslow Convalescent Home. Sergeant Harper would have been 24 years of age had he lived until May 7.

Mrs. Harper has another son serving with the London Regiment in Egypt, and her husband is also serving with the Beds. Regiment.

The sympathy of the townspeople will be extended to Mrs. Harper in her bereavement.

Having gone through so much action with the regiment, he was wounded again in the big German push which commenced on March 21st 1918. His battalion, as part of the 116th Brigade, 39th Division fought as they retired from near St Quentin on the 22nd March to Rosieres on 27th before they were withdrawn. Sergeant **William Harper** was severely wounded in the head on March 25th and died on April 11th, aged one month short of 24 years in one of the many large hospitals at Rouen, many miles behind the lines. He is buried in the St Sever Cemetery extension in Rouen, plot IX, row H, grave 12B. His mother, living at 17 Grove Road. received comforting letters from the hospital chaplain and the sister who nursed him. Poor Mrs Harper had her husband and another son away serving their country.

Arthur Pangbourne Hawkins

Date of Birth: 15-10-1882
First School: St Saviour's Infant
Hitchin Boys' British School
Date of Admission: 2-6-1890
Parents: George (a salesman) and Matilda
Address on admission: Bucklersbury
Left school: 13-6-96
Occupation: ?

Middlesex cap badge

1891 Census details

Living at 6 Bucklersbury, George, 49 (born in Paddington) was a clothier and his wife Matilda was 40. They had George W. 19, a gentleman's outfitter, Percy J. 14, Oscar J. 12, Emily E.10 and **Arthur P.** 8. They were born in the town.

1901 Census details

George was 59 and his wife 52. James was 22 (was he the Oscar J. from 1891?) He was a clothier's clerk. **Arthur** was 17 and again worked in the family business at 6 Bucklersbury and Elizabeth was 19 (was she the Emily E. from the 1891 census?)

1911 Census details

George, 69 and Matilda, 63 had two children still at home. These were

Arthur Pangbourne Hawkins

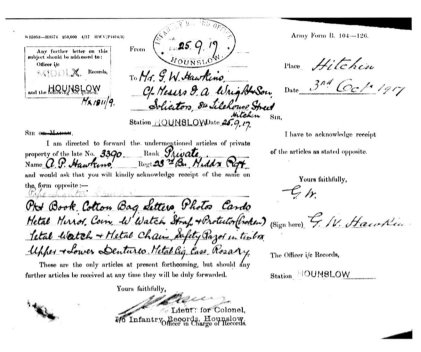

The sad list of his personal effects returned to his grieving parents

Arthur 28 a shop assistant in the family clothing business (later recorded as 'Dealers in Unredeemed Pledges' or pawnbrokers) and Emily 30. They had been married for 40 years, and had had 7 children, 6 of whom were still living. Their dwelling in Bucklersbury had 6 rooms.

Military details

Arthur's service records have survived, so much can be gleaned from these. He enlisted in Bedford on June 6th 1916 where he had his medical.

He was recorded as being 33 years of age and 5 foot 5 inches tall, weighing 119 lbs. His girth measurement was 35 inches (this was supposed to be the minimum!) with an expansion of 2 inches so he was a slight man.

Remembered

He had many teeth missing. He was put into the 23rd Battalion Middlesex Regiment (known as the 2nd Football Battalion, a 'Bantam' unit)

He became Private F/3390 and after initial training in England he went over to France on October 12th 1916. Training there for him was done at Etaples.

He joined the battalion 'in the field' on February 2nd 1917 and was seriously wounded just 2 months later on April 2nd 1917 in preparatory work for the forthcoming battle of Messines. He died the same day and was buried at Dickebusch New Military Cemetery, plot A, row A, grave 32. This is S.W. of Ypres in Belgium. I visited his grave with several Western Front Association friends on an autumn evening in 2013 to pay my respects and share his story.

Pte. **Arthur Hawkins** was in service for 128 days in Great Britain and 173 with the B.E.F. in France/Belgium making 301 days in total. He was 34 years old. The photograph of him kindly given by Mr. Peter Hawkins shows his youth.

From the service records it seems that his personal effects were sent to his father C/O F. A. Wright and Son, Solicitors, 84 Tilehouse Street Hitchin. This sad list included his upper and lower dentures, a mirror, razor, photos, letters, rosary, pipe lighter and crucifix.

Harry Hawkins (cousin of Percy Hawkins)

Date of Birth: 27-11-1893
First School: Hitchin British Infants' School
Hitchin Boys' British School
Date of Admission: 1-5-1901
Parents: Harry or Henry (plumber) and Lucy
Address on admission: Thorpe's Yard, Queen Street
Left school: 23-1-1908   Occupation: Errand boy

The cap badge of the Gloucestershires

1901 Census details

The family was living at 6 Thorpe's Yard, Queen Street. Father Harry 40, an 'oil and colourman's labourer and mother Lucy, 43 had Emily, 17 (crossed out in the census) Nellie, 15 and **Harry,** 7 . It was said that they were all born in Hitchin.

1911 Census details

The family was now living at 16 Exchange Yard, Market Place, in 4 rooms. Harry was 50 and a labourer, his wife Lucy was 53 and now was said to have been born at Therfield, Nr. Royston. Emily was back aged 26 and a domestic

Thorpe's yard where Harry lived at no. 6 in 1901

servant whilst Nellie, 25 and **Harry 17** were servant and house boy at the Boys' Grammar School. According to the details they had lost 6 children!

From newspaper reports it seems that **Harry** first worked at Spencer's Boot and Shoe shop at 38 Bucklersbury then at Boot's Chemist shop in Letchworth. He was a keen member of the Adult School and was said to be a good actor. From comments there, it seems that he was a very likeable lad who also was formerly a member of the Church Lads' Brigade and a Sunday School teacher for five years at St Mary's Church.

Military details

Harry enlisted in Letchworth in the Hertfordshire Regiment (4614) but, according to the medal roll entitlement he moved into the 1/4th Gloucestershire Regiment (39551) and because he was awarded 2 medals we know that he did not go abroad until after the beginning of 1916. He was in the 144th Brigade, 48th Division.

His brigade was holding the line on August 14th 1917 when the 145th were engaged with the enemy ahead of them to the south west of St Julien which is to the north of Ypres in Belgium. L.Cpl. **Harry Hawkins** was fatally wounded, aged 23 on that dreadful day (according to newspaper reports) with many others and this was said to be the low point for morale on the Western Front in August 1917. This was the infamous Passchendaele battle. He is buried in the

New Irish Farm Cemetery, plot I, row C, grave 15 where his death is recorded as 15th. This cemetery was started in August 1917 so his was one of the first burials amongst the 73 originals in the centre. The rest of the cemetery was used after the Armistice for battlefield collected burials. It was named after the nearby Irish Farm and is now surrounded by agricultural land but bounded by busy roads and within sight of

Impressive entrance to Irish Farm Cemetery

21st century wind turbines and industrial sites; a haven of peace. 'Thy Will Be Done' was his family's inscription.

Percy E. Hawkins (cousin of Harry Hawkins)

Date of Birth: 6-3-1889
First School: Hitchin British Infants' School
Hitchin Boys' British School
Date of Admission: 10-6-1895
Parents: Isaac (Yard-keeper) and Fanny
Address on admission: Telegraph Terrace [Kershaw's Hill]
Left school: 17-7-1903   Occupation: ?

The badge of Percy's regiment

1891 Census details
The family was living at 1 Wymondley Road. Father, Isaac 34, was a builder's yard foreman and his wife Fanny was 34. Isaac A. was 9, Leonard, 7, **Percy E.** was 2 and Bernard was 7 months. They were all born in Hitchin.

Further research showed that Isaac (Senior) was the brother of Harry Hawkins, the father of young Harry who was also killed in W.W.1.

1901 Census details
Isaac was now said to be 42 and his wife Fanny had died because he was now married to 27 year old Rebecca (née Freeman) who had been born in Royston. Leonard was 17 and a builder's labourer, **Percy** was 12, Bernard was 10 and Rex, 5 had arrived. They were living at 1 Taylor's Hill.

The couple had married in the final quarter of 1898 when in fact Fanny's death was registered.

1911 Census details

Living at 5 West Alley, Isaac, who was now 53, was a bird dealer. Rebecca was 37. Bernard was 20 and a tailor's porter. Rex at 15 was an errand boy in a private house and Cissy who was 13, Gertrude 7 and Hilda 5 had been born.

Military details

According to the newspaper report of October 12th 1916 (announcing his death on September 4th 1916) **Percy** had gone to live in Canada around 1906 making him very young to emigrate and it would seem that Bernard followed him out there. Before leaving Hitchin he worked in a distillery. In Canada he was making good progress working at the Regina Food Stores. He was married to Annie and had one child and was said to be well liked. They were living at 1737 Empress Street, Regina, British Columbia.

Percy Hawkins enlisted in Canada on September 17th 1915 and came to England for training in October 1915. On the attestation papers, his birth was recorded as March 12th 1890 which is different to the British Schools admission register, but it is definitely the same pupil so a mistake has occurred in transcription. He was recorded as being 5 feet 5 inches with blue eyes, light brown hair and a fair complexion. Whilst training in England he visited his Hitchin family twice.

He was Private 427648 in the 13th Battalion Canadian Infantry (Quebec Regiment) part of the 3rd Canadian Brigade in the 1st Canadian Division.

On the morning of September 4th 1916 Australian troops had attempted to take a German trench called Fabeck Graben near Mouquet Farm which was east of Thiepval. Later in the afternoon the 13th Canadians arrived and more came the next day. The enemy were then forced back with grenades and a barricade was erected. The Canadians during that period suffered heavy artillery fire and numerous counter attacks.

The following, from "The 13th Battalion Royal Highlanders" by R.C. Featherstonhaugh describes that 'trying' day in detail.

September 4th was a trying day for all the companies. Shelling was almost continuous and rain in the morning did not add to the men's comfort. No. 1 Coy. had received no rations for over 24 hours, but foraged about and discovered some excellent coffee in huge glass bottles, a souvenir left behind by the enemy when the Australian attack drove them out. This, with their own and German emergency rations, kept the men from feeling the absence of the regular rations too acutely.

No. 2 Coy. also suffered from shortage of food on this day, as well as from enemy shelling, which was persistent and accurate.

At night connection with No. 3 Coy. was definitely established. No. 3 also connected up with No. 4 during the night so that, by day break on the 5th, the Battalion was acting as a co-ordinated unit once more.

At 6 o clock in the morning a Red Cross flag appeared between the lines on No. 1 Coy's front and German stretcher bearers began to carry in their wounded. These bearers were unmolested by the Canadians, who took advantage of the situation to remove some of their own casualties. During this "armistice," Major Lovett noticed that several wounded Germans, eluding their own bearers, slipped into his trench and surrendered. This suggested to him that the morale of the German troops opposite him might not be of the highest order and that an attempt to induce them to surrender might be worth while.

Accordingly, as soon as the Red Cross Flag was withdrawn, Lovett and an Australian sergeant advanced to a position half way between the lines and tried to induce the Germans to come out. A measure of success seemed to be rewarding this move until a German officer appeared and promptly opened fire, his example being immediately followed by all his men. With a crash of rifle fire from their trenches, the Royal Highlanders endeavoured to drive the Germans under cover and give the daring negotiators a chance to escape. In this effort the men of No. 1 Coy. were only partially successful. Lovett got in, but the Australian sergeant was shot and instantly killed.

Following this incident enemy artillery fire increased and about 1 pm word was passed up from the right that Germans could be seen pouring up their communication trenches

as if for a heavy attack. The Lahore Artillery, supporting the Canadians, also received this information and laid down a heavy barrage which apparently broke the enemy attack before it could develop. As if in reply to this, the

The mourning 'Mother of Canada' at Vimy Ridge

Vimy Ridge Memorial

German artillery redoubled its fire and pounded No. 1 Coy's trench heavily. By this time some sixty per cent, of the Company had become casualties and to this total, additions were being made with unpleasant frequency. Major Lovett suffered his third wound of the war, an injury which held him in a London hospital for the three months that followed, while Lieut. Carmichael and Coy. Sergt.-Major Bullock, both of whom had distinguished themselves throughout the engagement, were also wounded. In the evening

Remembered

Lieut. C. D. Llwyd, who had fought most courageously, led the weary and famished remnant of the Company back into reserve.

Pte. **Percy Hawkins** was killed on that dreadful day and his body was not found so his name is alongside 11,284 others on the impressive Vimy Ridge Memorial to the Missing of Canada. He was 27.

Justus Alexander Hill

Date of Birth: 21-9-1890
First School: St Saviour's
Hitchin Boys' British School
Date of Admission: 17-5-1898
Parents: Widowed mother Emma
Address on admission: Ickleford Road
Left school: 7-7-1905   Occupation: Printer

1891 Census details

The family was living at 12 Ickleford Road. Father Samuel 36, (born in Buckinghamshire) was a butcher and his wife Emma was 40 (born Baldock) They had Jennie, 9 (born in Surrey) as were Rowland M. 8 and Daisy E. 6. Ann F. 5, Henry W. 2 and **Justus A.** 6 months were all born in Hitchin.

1901 Census details

In the same house ten years later sadly Samuel had died and the widowed Emma 50, had taken in boarders William Harding, 58 a cabinet maker and Stephen J. King, 25 a carpenter. Ann 15, was still at home as were William H, 12 and **Alexander J,** 10 (their Christian names were recorded in reverse on this census!) Harriet M, 7 and Dorothy E, 5 had been born, suggesting that Samuel had died after 1896.

1911 Census details

Mother Emma now 60 was now living at 20 Benslow Lane, 'living on her own means' with her two youngest daughters. Harriet M. was recorded as a dressmaker. According to the census they were living in 2 rooms (not counting the kitchen, scullery, bathroom etc. even if indeed they had these luxuries). **Justus Alexander** was really elusive on this census but eventually found on board the Royal Navy ship HMS "Royalist" at Queenstown, Ireland on the night of the census, April 2nd 1911 when he was aged 20.

Military details

Justus Hill was on board HMS "Monmouth" in November 1914 off the coast of Chile, South America. On the 'Coronel' website can be found reproduced the letters sent home from a young Royal Marine bandsman to his mother when he

Plymouth Naval Memorial

HMS Monmouth

Map of the Battle of Coronel

was on board the same ship. These give a graphic account of the journey and the good food on board which our **Justus** would have been preparing. **Justus** was Cook's mate II Class M/3422 when the ship was involved in the dreadful Battle of Coronel. He died so early in the war and so far from home alongside all the crew on November 1st 1914. He is remembered on the Plymouth Naval Memorial, Panel 4. He was 24.

Frederick Hinstridge

Date of Birth: 23-10-1893
First School: Hitchin British Infants' School
Hitchin Boys' British School
Date of Admission: 21-5-1900
Parents: William (a house painter) and Rebecca
Address on admission: 12 Union
Road [Oughtonhead Way]
Left school: 31-3-1907
Occupation: Errand boy

*Royal Garrison
Artillery badge*

1901 Census details

Father William 36, a house painter (born in Stepney) and his wife Rebecca 37 had Thomas Albert 12, **Frederick** 7 and Florence Ethel 3 and they were living in Union Road.

1911 Census details

The family was now living at Charlton near Hitchin in 5 rooms. William 45, was still a house painter and had been married to Rebecca 46, for 23 years. Thomas Albert at 22 had the same job as his father but **Frederick** now 17 was a Tea Blender at a grocery shop. Florence was 12 and William, 9 and

HASLER W. G.
HIGGINS J.
HILL F. W.
HINSTRIDGE F.
HOLDHAM F.
HONEYBALL A.
HOUSTON F. W.
HUMPHREYS S.
JONES W.
KIDSON H

One of over 54,000 names

Elsie, 7 had been born. Sadly they stated that 2 children had died.

Military details

We know that he enlisted in Hitchin and as there are no service records surviving it is difficult to tell when he went across to the battlefields but certainly it was

The Menin Gate with Ypres visible through the arch

after December 1915 as he was awarded only the Victory and War medals. It seems that the poor lad was killed after less than 3 months in the service of the 20th Trench Mortar Battery, Royal Garrison Artillery on March 14th 1916 at the age of 22. Gunner **Frederick Hinstridge** 66019, is commemorated on Panel 9 of the Menin Gate Memorial to the Missing at Ypres in Belgium.

Bertram Hunt (brother of Frederick)

Date of Birth: 19-10-1889
First School: Hitchin British Infants' School
Hitchin Boys' British School
Date of Admission: 7-5-1897
Parents: Thomas and Esther
Address on admission: Davis Alley (off Queen Street)
Left school: 11-9-1903
Occupation: "Gone to work"

M.G.C. cap badge

1891 Census details

Father Thomas 36 (a plumber's labourer) and his wife Esther 31 were living at 16 Corrie's Yard with their children, Arthur 13, George 7, William 4 and **Bertie** 1. They were all born in Hitchin.

1901 Census details

The family was living at 7 Davis Alley where father Thomas, 47, a plumber was married to Hester (sic) 42. Their children were George 17, a 'straw tier', William 14, **Bertram** 10, Frederick 9 and Lily 6.

1911 Census details

The census states that they were living at 53 Queen Street in 5 rooms. Thomas (now Tom) was still a labourer in plumbing, Hester (now Ester) was 53. George, 28 was a distiller, William, 24 was a 'carman' in hay and straw, **Bert,** 21 was a fruiterer, Lily was 17, Frederick 19, was a shop boy in groceries and Violet had arrived, aged 10.

Military details

Bertram Hunt enlisted on 15-11-1915 at Hitchin, giving his address as 53 Queen Street, occupation "Hawker", age 27 years 1 month and next of kin (mother) Esther Hunt, of the same address. He was known to have worked also for F.Furr the fish merchant in Bridge Street after his time as a fruiterer. He was 5'9" tall and weighed 140 lbs. He said he had 2 brothers and two sisters.

He joined the Bedfordshire Regiment at Bedford, and carried out basic military training there. He was transferred to the M.G.C. April 12th 1916 and almost certainly went to Belton Park, Grantham for specialist training.

An extract from the diary of a certain Herbert Minchin of the M.G.C.states that "The training was very hard, there was much carrying to do and heavy work which explained why only fit men were picked for the Corps. The Vickers gun itself when filled with water weighs 40lbs; then there is the heavy tripod which has to be carried by one leg over each shoulder and the trail leg down the back. This is two men's work and it was impossible to carry them far without a rest. Others carried the spare parts box and belt boxes each carrying one belt with 200 rounds of ammunition." (from document Minchin H.I. 06-55-1 in the Documents Dept. of the Imperial War Museum)

I have a special interest in soldier Hunt as I am a member of the Machine Gun Corps Old Comrades Association and have been with them on a battlefield trip. I also attend the Annual Observance Service in St Wolfram's Church, Grantham where their colours and Book of Remembrance can be seen.

Bertram's service records revealed the following details:

To France (1st time) June 25th 1916 - joined 62 Coy. (Somme sector)

M.G.C. Memorial, St. Wolfram's Church, Grantham, Lincolnshire

July 14th 1916 (Battle of Bazentin Ridge) - shell shock. Sent to UK July 16th 1916 - in hospital at Northampton until October 22nd 1916 (Granted leave August 26th -September 4th) Sent back out to France (2nd time) January 20th 1917, joined 51 Coy. Probably saw action 1st Battle of the Scarpe 12-April 14 1917, 2nd Battle of the Scarpe 23-April 24th 1917, Capture & Defence of Rouex 13-May 16 1917, Died of

Sunken Road Cemetery

wounds in 51 Field Ambulance Station on July 13 1917 aged 27.

Pte. **Bertram Hunt** who was 27, is buried in Sunken Road Cemetery, Fampoux plot 1, row B, grave 6. This is a beautiful cemetery and an English rose was casting an evening shadow on his headstone when I visited him on September 8th 2012 There is a note about his death in the unit war diary:

War Diary July 13th 1917: *"Enemy had two direct hits on trenches occupied by gun teams. We had the following casualties, No 8 gun in CORK TRENCH, 84546 Pte W. Mathias killed, 31506 Pte B Hunt died of wounds".*

Private Matthias is buried six graves along the same row at I, B, 12

The Newspaper report of July 21st 1917 describes him having been severely wounded on 13th and expired after reaching the dressing station on the same day. The Rev. W. Edwin Fleming of the 6th. Dorset Regiment said that he was with him at his death as was Private J. Stevens R.A.M.C. an old friend and school fellow. Research reveals that this was probably Jabez Stevens (known as Jack) and he lived at 2 Whinbush Road. Hitchin. The chaplain buried Bertram that evening.

Frederick Hunt (brother of Bertram)

Date of Birth: 29-7-1891
First School: Hitchin British Infants' School
Hitchin Boys' British School
Date of Admission: 29-5-1899
Parents: Thomas (a plumber)and Hester
Address on admission: 7 Davis' Alley (off Queen Street)
Left school: 3-8-1905
Occupation: Errand boy
See census details of his brother above.

Military details

Frederick enlisted in Hitchin. It would appear that he was working for Messrs. J Gatward and Sons at the time. He first joined the Bedfordshire Regiment (3582) then was transferred to the 1/4th Essex Regiment 201172 and his medals entitlement shows that he went out to war after training at the beginning of 1916 when that regiment was in Egypt having already been

1917 Herts Express

involved in the dreadful Gallipoli campaign of 1915. He was killed in the first battle of Gaza 26th-27th March 1917.

His battalion was part of the 161st Brigade, 54th Division which, having crossed the Wadi Ghuzze and occupying the Sheikh Abbas Ridge, attacked the Turks who were being hard pressed to the north and north-east of Gaza. These Turks on Green Hill had inflicted severe casualties all day by their machine-gun fire on our troops. The culminating point in the day's operations was reached between 4pm. and 5 pm. when the 4th and 5th Essex Battalions

advanced rapidly and successfully on Green Hill and enabled the whole of our line to advance. The Turks fled to Gaza. Pte.**Frederick Hunt** was killed during this attack and is buried in the Gaza War Cemetery plot XXVI, row C, grave no. 9. He was 25.

After receiving the sad news of **Frederick's** death, the widowed mother (for Tom had died between 1911 and 1917) would again, four months later, receive the dreaded telegram telling her of the death of another son, Bertram.

Essex Regiment cap badge

George James

Date of Birth: 31-3-1889
First School: Hitchin British Infants' School
Hitchin Boys' British School
Date of Admission: 10-6-1895
Parents: Daniel (a bricklayer) and Mary Ann
Address on admission: Bedford Road
Left school: 20-2-1903
Occupation: Oil shop errand boy

*The emblem of The
Buffs, (The East Kent
Regiment)*

1891 Census details

The family was living at 37 Bedford Road and Daniel 34, (born in Hitchin) was
a bricklayer. His wife Mary Ann 37, (born in Offley) was mother to John 13, a
grocer's errand boy, Kate 9, Samuel 8, Ruth 4 and **George**, 2.

1901 Census details

They were now living at 30 Bedford Road. Daniel 45, was still a bricklayer and
Mary Ann had had 5 more children! Samuel James 18 was now a bricklayer
too, Ruth 14, was a laundress, **George** was 12, Eva 8, Daniel 6, Arthur 4, Mary
Ann 2 and Gladys Mary 2 months.

1911 Census details

George was now in the barracks of the 4th Dragoon Guards at Steyning,
Sussex as a 22 year old private.(April 3rd 1911)

Research shows that he married Catherine Elizabeth Kent in the Royston area
between April and June 1915.

George's Grave

Military details

There are no service records remaining but
from his medal entitlement we know that he
went on active service after the beginning of
1916. **Private James**, 35626 was in the Buffs
(The East Kent Regiment)

His battalion was part of the 55th Brigade,
18th Division. The 18th Division was
involved in so much action and praised for
its bravery. The Division took active roles in
the battles of the Somme, Arras and Ypres.

The 11th November 1918, when hostilities
ceased, saw them in the villages around

Le Cateau. The units forming Kitchener's New Armies were the first for disbandment so the 18th Division did not take part in the march into Germany. From December 1918 to March 1919 all hands were employed clearing up the battlefield, a very necessary and at times dangerous undertaking. The 7th Buffs were singularly unlucky, having 10 men killed by the explosion of a live shell. It is likely that George was one of these on December 17th.

How unlucky, to go all through the conflict and to be killed after hostilities had ceased. He was 29 years old and was buried in Honnechy British Cemetery, plot 1, row B, grave 1 with a touching inscription at the base of his headstone 'Abide With Me'. When I visited I discovered that the wrong year had been engraved on his headstone and have informed the Commonwealth War Graves Commission.

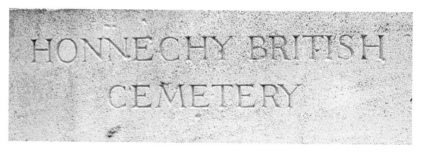

Honnechy British Cemetery

Edgar Philip King

Date of Birth: 2-8-1883
First School: St Saviour's Infant
Hitchin Boys' British School
Date of Admission: 8-6-1891
Parents: Arthur John (G.N.R. carpenter) and Ellen
Address on admission: 46 Nightingale Road
Left school: 26-11-1895   Occupation: ?

Royal Fusiliers cap badge

1891 Census details

The family was living at 46 Nightingale Road, Arthur was 31 (born in Godmanchester, Hunts.) and Ellen, his wife 31, (born in Ickleford) had 4 children. **Edgar Philip** 7 was a scholar, Francis C. was 4, Gertrude H 2, Beatrice was 8 months.

1901 Census details

The family was now living at 6 St Anne's Road. Arthur was 40, Ellen 39, **Edgar** 17 was a 'domestic groom,' Francis 14, was a milk boy, Gertrude was 12, Beatrice 10, Arthur 8, Mabel 6, George 4 and Leslie 1. Also Alice Jeeves 38, Ellen's sister was staying with them with her child Tilly, 3.

1911 Census details

Arthur now 51 and Ellen 50 had been married for 28 years and were living at the same address in what they declared was 6 roomed accommodation. They had had 10 children and all were still living.

Edgar Philip 27 was a house painter and living at home but the next 4 siblings had moved out though the parents mistakenly put their details on the census form and crossed them out. So we know that Francis married in 1909, Gertrude married also in 1909, Beatrice was a dressmaker and Arthur junior was a coachman. Mabel, 16 was a dressmaker living at home, George 13, Leslie 11, and Albert E. were at school and Stanley was 6.

Military details

Edgar had by now married Annie Florence of Hinchingbrooke Lodge, Huntingdon. He is said to have been resident and enlisted in Hitchin. No service records remain but he was awarded two medals so we know that he went over to France after the beginning of 1916. He enlisted in the Essex Battalion in April 1916 and was originally 37440 in the Training Reserve battalion but was transferred on December 9th into the Royal Fusiliers as G/52706 in the 26th Battalion. This was known as the Bankers' Battalion and was raised by the Lord Mayor and City of London from bank clerks and accountants on July 17th 1915.

On their move to Belgium they were concentrated near Steenwerck, where they began familiarisation with trench warfare in the areas of Ploegsteert and the Douve valley, south of Ypres. They remained here until August 1916, when they moved to

Edgar King

Edgar, back row left

the Somme, and took part in the Battle of Flers-Courcelette. The Division remained in the line, pushing on to Courcelette over the next few days before coming out for a rest and re-fit. They then fought at the Battle of Le Transloy.

On June 7th 1917 Lance Corporal **Edgar King** was killed aged 33 on the first day of the Battle of Messines (7-14th June, 1917) his battalion being part of the 124th Brigade, 41st Infantry Division. The objective of he and his chums as they attacked on the 7th June was the private access road which ran in a straight line from the St Eloi - Oostaverne road to the White Château. They had been told that it was a bit of a stumbling block and strongly fortified. Our artillery had prepared the Germans well for them and as our artillery barrage lifted the Bankers rushed in and captured the position with very little resistance and before large numbers of the enemy, who had been sheltering in strong concrete dug-outs, were able to come out and fight. They captured between 300 & 400 Germans who surrendered.

There was one exception to this surrender - one isolated enemy machine-gun crew put up some strong resistance before being knocked out. Perhaps **Edgar** was killed by this or in the general attack. A soldier in hospital wrote to Edgar's parents to say that he had last seen their son wounded in a shell hole. His body was not recovered immediately and a month later his parents were informed that he was missing. Four more of their sons were also serving their country it

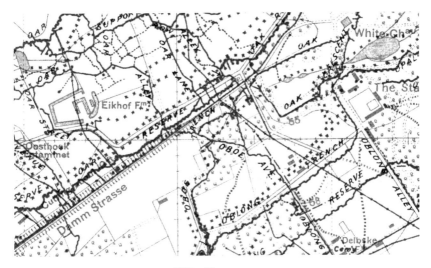

White Chateau map

was reported in the press. One narrowly missed death in a Canadian Military hospital that was devastated by an air raid in May 1918. I have 4 press cuttings with more details.

It was not until May of the following year that Edgar's widow who lived in Hinchingbrooke, was informed that death had been assumed. His body was indeed recovered and 33 year old L.Cpl. **Edgar King** is buried in Voormezeele Enclosure No. 3 Cemetery, Belgium in plot 13, row H, grave 7. I visited on an October evening in 2013 as the evening shadows lengthened. National committee members of the Western Front Association joined me to pay their respects and to hear his story. At the base of his headstone was engraved 'Peace Perfect Peace'. Also in this cemetery is the grave of 2nd Lt. George Llewelyn Lewis upon whom J.M. Barrie based his character Peter Pan. **Edgar's** great nephew, Brendan King, has kindly provided his family photographs received from Edgar's niece Lesley Anne Knight.

William Kingsley

Date of Birth: 1-3-1877
First School: ?
Hitchin Boys' British School
Date of Admission: 12.7.1886

Parents: Elizabeth. (no father named)
Address on admission: Union Workhouse
Left school: 5-12-1890   Occupation: ?

1881 Census details

William was living with his mother and grandparents in Davis Alley, off Queen Street. Grandfather Edward 50, his wife Edith 36 and Elizabeth 25 were there with young **William** 4 (grandson) and Herbert 14 and Henry 10 (said to be sons- in- law!).

1886 **William** was admitted to the British School with a Union Workhouse address and left in 1890.

1891 Census details

Cannot be found.

1894 **William** joined the army. His service records have survived.

1901 Census details

William 24, as head of household was living at 10, St John's Lane with his mother 45 and sister Louisa 18.

1911 Census details

Living at 16 Sunnyside, **William** now 33 was the head of the household. His mother Elizabeth was 53 and Louisa 27 and Harry 4 (nephew) with Eva 2 (niece) were living with him.

Military details

William enlisted in Bedford on July 31st 1894 and went into the West Yorkshire Regiment as Private 4180 (details confirmed in service records).

William's details

☆ Height, 5 feet 8 inches. Weight, 149lbs.
☆ Hair and eyes, brown.
☆ Chest, 35 ½ inches.
☆ Religion, C. of E.
☆ Distinguishing marks, scar on right side of head and scald on abdomen.
☆ Next of kin was recorded as sister Louisa now living at Newtown Road. Birmingham.

September 17 1894 there was a Board of Enquiry at Aldershot concerning **William** who, it was stated, was saying that he was unfit for duty because he'd had an accident on the gymnastics bar. This had been witnessed but the board found him fit for duty!

He was posted to his regiment on October 18th 1894 but it would seem he was found to be 'lazy and inattentive in the ranks' and was confined to barracks on two occasions.

Then on December 15th he went 'absent without leave' taking with him his army greatcoat, valued at £1.0.3d. an army cape valued at 7/- and his army waist belt, valued at 4/9d.together with all his personal belongings. He had been warned that he was due to go on 'foreign service'. This all came out at another Board of Enquiry on Feb. 4th 1895.

Remembered today

We do not know what happened to him as the next time he appears is in the 1911 census living at 16 Sunnyside and working on a farm as a labourer.

The Great War

He joined the army again and went over to France with the 8th Battalion Bedfordshire Regiment as Private, 18301 on January 20th 1916.

The 8th Battalion was in the area of Ypres in the early months of the year undergoing intensive training but were also involved in trench work and suffered terribly in a massed bombardment in April.

They were moved down to the Somme area in early August to back up battalions

William's grave

who had really suffered in the early days of the Somme battle that began on July 1st. As a service battalion they were much involved in working parties, digging and repairing trenches and were very vulnerable to enemy fire.

It was on August 21st as seen in the war diary that Pte. **William Kingsley** was killed aged 39 and a comrade was injured. He is buried in Mesnil Cemetery Extension, plot 1, row A, grave 20 which is 6km.north west of Albert and about 4 km. from where he was killed. He seemed to have had a sad start in life with a period in the workhouse then no doubt he joined the army to get away but he did not cope with the disciplined life there. He nevertheless died fighting for his country like so many others.

William Charles Lawson

Date of Birth: 12-12-1895
First School: Offley
Hitchin Boys' British School
Date of Admission: 27-10-1908
Parents: James and Caroline
Address on admission: 28 Periwinkle Lane
Left school: 22-12-1909
Occupation: Builder's clerk

The Trio would have been sent to his next of kin

1901 Census details

The family was living at Greenford Road, Greenford, Middlesex where father James 38, (born in Southsea, Hants) was a domestic gardener. His wife Caroline was 39 and born in Romsey and they had Mabel 10, (born in Romsey), Alice 8, (born in Thornham, Sussex), **William** 5, (born in Braintree, Essex), Dorothy 2, (born in Greenford), likewise Jesse, who was only 3 weeks old.

1911 Census details

The family was now living in Hitchin at 28 Periwinkle Lane. James was recorded as 45 and his wife 44, which does not tally with the last census. Often, mistakes can be found in censuses, either by the enumerator or 'rounding up or down' was done. They stated that they had been married for 21 years and were living in 5 rooms but had lost 1 child. **William** 15 was now an under clerk in a timber business. Dorothy was 12 and Jesse 10.

Military details

William volunteered in Hitchin in September 1914 and as Private Lawson 14800 was in the 1st Battalion Bedfordshire Regiment when he went overseas in April 1915.

His battalion was immediately in action on Hill 60, south of Ypres, Belgium. This high point was much fought over and changed hands many times with great loss of life on both sides. Between 19th and 21st April they held the hill against counter-attacks and very heavy shelling before being relieved after 3 days and moving back behind the lines. During this short time the Bedfords had 400 casualties killed, wounded or missing. They took over the trenches again on April 25th and the enemy attacked them again on May 1st using gas to a devastating degree. The remains of the battalion was driven off the hill by the Germans on May 5th.

William, just 19, died of wounds it was said on May 1st. Either he was wounded in that short dreadful battle or he died as a result of the gas poisoning on that day. The poor lad was killed just one month after going to the front.

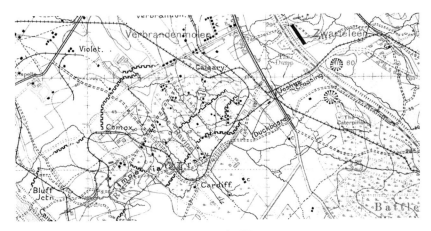

Hill 60, south of Ypres

Pte. **William Lawson** is commemorated on the Menin Gate Memorial to the Missing in Ypres, Panels 31 and 33, alongside about 55,000 others.

George Young Lewis

Date of Birth: 30-9-1887
First School: ?
Hitchin Boys' British School
Date of Admission: 10-6-1895
Parents: Samuel (a fellmonger dealing in sheepskins) and Selina
Address on admission: Grove Road
Left school: 10-5-1901   Occupation: Bookstall, GNR

1891 Census details

The family was living at 7 Anderson's Row, off Florence Street Samuel 29, was a skinner of fur. Selina (née Muncey) his wife, was 27 and their children were **George** 3 and Nellie 2 months. An Alice Cowper 11, sister, was living with the family. They were all born in Hitchin.

1901 Census details

They were now living at 8 Verulam Road, and Samuel and family were listed with the Young Lewis surname though the earlier census just said Lewis. He was still a fur skinner in Tempsford and Selina had **George** 13, Nellie 10, May 9, John 4 and Harry 3 to care for.

1911 Census details

The family was still living at the same address but **George** who would now have been 23 was missing from the household so perhaps he had already emigrated in order to seek his fortune.

The details now say that Samuel was born in Irthlingborough, Northants. Nellie 20, was a dressmaker, May 17, a milliner, John 14, was a bookstall newsboy for W.H. Smith and Harry 13, was at school.

Military details

George now appears at Sulphur Creek on the north coast of Tasmania and is married. 'He had emigrated to Tasmania where he lived for eleven years and was in business with his father-in-law as a nurseryman, having previously been employed as a chauffeur' (David Baines).

☆ We know from the Australian Archives that **George Young Lewis** underwent a medical on March 3rd 1916 when he was declared fit for service.

☆ He was 28 years 5 months and weighed 10st 2lbs with a height of 5 feet 6 ½ inches.

☆ He had fair hair and complexion and bluish grey eyes.

☆ He was the husband of Ivy Clarice Rumley Lewis and they lived at Sulphur Creek on the north coast of Tasmania.

☆ He is recorded as enlisting on March 29th 1916 at Claremont, a pretty Hobart suburb on the Derwent River where there was an army training facility in W.W.1.

As Sapper (Tunneller) 5770 in the 2nd Company, Australian Tunnelling Corps, he left Melbourne for Plymouth (U.K.) on HMAT " Ulysses" as part of the Australian Tunnelling Companies 1916 Reinforcements on 25th October 1916. He remained in training in England then went to Etaples in France and from

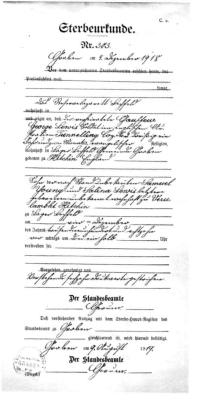

His German death certificate

there to Belgium in early 1917. His company relieved the Canadians at The Bluff in January 1917 and moved to Nieuport on the coast in the same month to construct subways for Operation Hush. They were involved in an enemy attack - Operation Strandfest - in this coastal sector in July 1917. This is where he was captured and taken to Lechfeld P.O.W. camp, Graben, Germany on July 10th.

Lechfeld was a training and exercise camp in southern Germany and it was here in 1914 that the young struggling artist Adolph Hitler and Rudolf Hess trained, having been recruited into the 16th Bavarian Reserve Infantry Regiment.

The following was gleaned from the Great War Forum online.

The camp contained a strafe or reprisal unit for NCOs who were pressured into volunteering for work, despite the provisions of the Hague Convention. In 1917 a group of 22 British NCOs including some Australians, was transferred there from Nuremberg and subjected to a harsh regime-deprived of Red Cross parcels for 2 months, denied cooking facilities etc but they refused to buckle. The commandant had formerly been an internee in England. Food was atrocious: 160 grams of bread per day, turnip water and occasional rations of dried black horsemeat. Corporal Fred Smith 1st Northamptonshire Regt. escaped with a Frenchman from an outside working party and made it to Switzerland in May 1918. Unsuccessful escapers faced 3-7 days in the "bivouac," a wire cage where the victim was kept in thin German issue clothing and fed on bread and water. The treatment of the Italians, Russians and Rumanians was particularly appalling. 580 Italians died from the results of cold, starvation and ill treatment in just 2 months. Little of the original camp remains today.

Sadly George died there of Grippe (Spanish Flu) on December 5th 1918 aged 31. Amazingly, in the Australian Archives (Canberra) which are available on the internet, there is a photograph of his funeral behind the church in Lechfeld taken by a fellow prisoner. In 1924 he was re-interred in Niederzwehren Cemetery, plot II, grave 8 where the family inscription reads, 'Without you we can do nothing, we three till we meet again'. His service records have of course survived in Australia and there are 67 pages, all on-line. Much information has been gleaned from them.

He had a daughter who was born on March 30th 1917. We know this from another set of records at the Australian Archives which hold 53 pages of letters going backwards and forwards from his wife Ivy to the Paymaster General asking for her allowances to be paid at the Penguin Post Office near Sulphur Creek. One wonders whether he ever knew about little Laurel Emily Young Lewis. Although Ivy at first was told he was missing, she then heard from the Red Cross and from England (presumably his family in Hitchin) that he was

AUSTRALIAN IMPERIAL FORCE.

B.R. Form No. 9.

BASE RECORDS OFFICE,
VICTORIA BARRACKS,
D.H. MELBOURNE, 15th Jan. 1918.

Dear Madam,

I now beg to advise you that Sapper G.Y. Lewis
has been reported prisoner of war, Germany "officially"
and is interned at Limburg, Germany.
His postal address will be :—

BRITISH PRISONER OF WAR, GERMANY,
No. 5770, Sapper G.Y. Lewis,
2nd Tunnelling Company,
Australian Imperial Force,
c/o Australian Red Cross Commissioners,
Abroad.

In the absence of further reports it is to be assumed that satisfactory progress is
being maintained, but anything later received will be promptly transmitted, it being
clearly understood that if no further advice is forwarded this department has no more
information to supply.

Yours faithfully,

J. M. LEAN, Major,
Officer in Charge, Base Records.

(Above) Wife informed of his imprisonment

(Below) His funeral service at Lechfeld P.O.W. Camp

a prisoner of war in Germany. She was eventually given her widow's allowance and that for her daughter. Laurel, I have found, later married a Gordon Leslie Bird and they had 2 children, a girl who died aged ten and a son David George Bird, the grandson of our soldier. I am trying to contact him.

Henry Walter Marchant

Date of Birth: 15-4-1892
First School: St Saviour's Infant
Hitchin Boys' British School
Date of Admission: 21-5-1900
Parents: Henry W. and Laura
Address on admission: 52 Radcliffe Road
Left school: 25-6-1906
Occupation: Doctor's errand boy

The 1914 Star trio would have been sent to Ellen

1901 Census details

Henry 35, was a railway porter, his wife Laura was 35 and they had Archibald 12, Agnes 10, **Henry** 8 and Hilda 5. They lived at 52 Radcliffe Road.

1911 Census details

They were still at the same address and Henry (Snr.) was a railway brakesman. Archibald was living elsewhere and they had lost a child but **Walter** 18, was a railway porter, Hilda 15, was an art needle maker, Marjorie was 7, Kathleen and Lawrence were 1.

1915

Walter married Ellen Daisy Chalkley and they had a child, Walter Ernest William (1917-1999).

Military details

Walter enlisted in Hertford in 1914 and was in France with the 1st Hertfordshire Regiment by November 6th suggesting that he was part of the territorial army unit based in Hertford. He qualified for the 1914 Star as well as the War and Victory medals. His first number was 2585 and his second 265531.

As can be seen from the war diary extract below he had a gruelling war and made it through to the final year.

Major Battles

The 1st/1st battalion served entirely on the Western Front throughout the war and was engaged in the following battles:

In 1914 they were lightly involved in The Battles of Ypres 1914 (also called The First Battle of Ypres).

In 1915 the battalion wasengaged during the Winter actions at Cuinchy in February, the Battle of Festubert in May and at the Battle of Loos in September.

In 1916 the battalion was engaged in the Battles of the Somme 1916, including being lightly involved in the Battle of the Ancre Heights in October, as well as in the Battle of the Ancre in November.

In 1917 the battalion was heavily engaged during the opening day of the Battles of Ypres 1917 (also called the Third Battle of Ypres and Passchendaele), when the battalion lost over 450 men during

52 Radcliffe Road Hitchin

their assault on St Julien, part of the Battle of Pilkem. They were also involved less heavily in the Battle of Langemarck in August, the Battle of the Menin Road and the Battle of Polygon Wood in September, as well as the Second Battle of Passchendaele in October.

During 1918, the battalion was again heavily engaged. During the First Battles of the Somme 1918 (also called the German Spring Offensives, Operation Michael and Kaiserschlacht), they were heavily involved in the Battle of St Quentin, the actions on the Somme crossings and the Battle of Rosieres in March.

Pte. **Henry Marchant** was killed in action aged 25 on 22nd March 1918 in the area of Aizecourt-les-Bas/VillersFaucon in the Somme sector, whilst being pushed back in the major German offensive which started on March 21st 1918 (St Quentin).

Corrections can be seen on his medals entitlement card

He left behind, his wife Ellen of New Council Cottages, Walkern Road, Stevenage and a young child, Walter. His body was not found and he is commemorated on the Pozieres Memorial to the Missing Panels 89-90. His name is alongside 14,600 names of the missing and there are 2,700 burials.

• • • ● ● ● • • •

Arthur William Minnis

Date of Birth: 7-3-1890
First School: St Saviour's Infant
Hitchin Boys' British School
Date of Admission: 23-5-1898
Parents: William (a horse-keeper) and Mary
Address on admission: 47 Bancroft
Left school: 6-3-1903   Occupation: Farm boy

1891 Census details

The family lived at 1 Walnut Tree Cottages (Bancroft). William 63, was a farm labourer and his wife Mary 28, was a straw plaiter. The children were recorded as Rose Minnis 12, Elsie V. 3 months and **Arthur** 1. (William and Mary had married in 1889.) Also resident was Ann Cannon, mother-in-law 65, a widow.

1897 on admission to the school, the address was given as 47 Bancroft.

1901 Census details

Now living at 41 Bancroft, William 72 and Mary 38, had **Arthur** 9 and Florence 8, at home.

1911 Census details

Still living at 41 Bancroft, **Arthur** 19, a farm labourer was at home with his old age pensioner father 81 and Mary 48. He subsequently married and lived in Florence Street.

Military details

Arthur enlisted on July 12th 1916 as 30901 in the 5th Battalion, Bedfordshire Regiment which was part of the 162nd Brigade 54th Division, (East Anglian). Before **Arthur's** time with them they had been in action in the 1915 Gallipoli campaign where their bravery gave them the name of the 'Yellow Devils'. When that finished in December, few remained and reinforcements were needed to fill the ranks. They were moved to Egypt to be 're-built' then had a 1 year posting to guard the Suez Canal. Their next action was in the advance to Gaza and then into Palestine.

Arthur was part of the new draft and was on the troopship the S.S. Aragon trying to land in Egypt when it was torpedoed off Alexandria and he and so many others lost their lives. (See the extract from The Bedfordshire Regiment's War Diary below).

The sinking of the S.S. Aragon, 30th December 1917

The S.S. Aragon goes down
Roll of Honour.
Men of the 5th Battalion who drowned at sea on the 30th December 1917.

Private 30901 Arthur William MINNIS

Born at Hitchin, enlisted from Bedford, resident of Hitchin. Drowned on the 30th December 1917 and remembered on the Chatby Memorial to the missing.

May you all rest in peace, knowing that your efforts are still remembered and your sacrifice honoured.

1917 was a dreadful year for the Allied powers, despite the gains made both on the Western Front and in the Eastern Mediterranean theatre. The Arras offensives in April were deemed a success, despite the usual high casualty rates, with the year's big push (the "Third Ypres" or "Passchendaele") achieving its objective but at a truly horrendous loss of life. The Russian Army had left the field after the

Sinking of S.S Aragon

revolution at home and the French Army all but mutinied, refusing to go on the offensive due to their horrific losses in attack after attack. Offensive operations were therefore left to the British and Empire forces, which almost broke their morale, in the mud around Passchendaele. As the year's carnage settled into the usual winter routines of simply holding the lines, a further set of disastrous losses awaited the British forces at the very end of 1917.

War Diary Extract

On the 30th December 1917, the Troopship S.S. Aragon arrived at Alexandria Harbour, having sailed from Marseilles on the 17th December. She was laden with around 2,700 troops bound for the conflicts raging in Palestine.

As she arrived in a convoy bound for the port, the rest of the ships sailed onwards to Alexandria and she lay up ten miles off shore, awaiting her escort. The 9588 tons of ocean liner drifted gently as she waited within sight of land but was torpedoed by the German Submarine and minelayer the UC-34.

The destroyer HMS Attack dashed to her rescue as she sunk quickly, as well as every

available ship within reach. Many of the men rescued were taken onto the HMS Attack and had just stripped their oil drenched clothes from their bodies and laid on the deck when she too was torpedoed by the same submarine, almost blowing her in two.

The following day – New Years Eve – just as the rescue was called off, fleet auxiliary craft HMS Osmanieh also hit a mine in the area, taking another 197 soldiers and nurses down with her.

610 of the 2,700 passengers on board the HMS Aragon were lost at sea, including 25 of the new draft bound for the 5th Battalion of the Bedfordshire regiment.'

Pte. **Arthur Minnis** is commemorated on the Chatby War Memorial in Egypt. He was 27.

Alfred Monk

Date of Birth: 12-5-1898
First School: Hitchin British Infants' School
Hitchin Boys' British School
Date of Admission: 1-5-1905
Parents: Henry and Mary A
Address on admission: 31 Hitchin Hill
Left school: 27-1-1913
Occupation: Motor Engineer

Royal Fusiliers cap badge

1901 Census details.

Living at 31 Hitchin Hill, father Henry 45, was a distillery labourer. His wife Mary A. was 45 and they had 7 children living at home. George was 14, William 12, Sarah 9, Alice 7, Richard 4, **Alfred** 2 and Lizzie 3 months.

1911 Census details

The family was now living at 1 Slip Yard, Queen Street and Harry 55, was a timber trade labourer. Richard 14, **Alfred** 12 and Petrolius 10, were still at home. They had had 13 children of whom 12 were still alive and they had been married for 30 years.

Military details

Alfred enlisted at 15 $^1/_2$ years at the outbreak of war in the Herts Regiment but was released as under age. At 18 he was called up and posted to the London Regiment (75967) then he transferred to the Royal Fusiliers. He went to France in about May 1918.

The newspaper report of Sept. 14th 1918 filled in many details. He was the youngest of 6 brothers, 5 of whom served in the Great War. The eldest had served in the Boer War as had two of those who served in the Great War.

Before joining the army **Alfred** was employed at the Electric Light Works in Whinbush Road and also at an ammunition factory in Letchworth.

He was wounded at the 2nd Battle of Bapaume in late August 1918. During August the Allies started to push back the Germans for the final time, the start of the Advance to Victory and the last 100 days. By the 13th August his division had advanced astride the Corbie-Bray road on the Morlancourt Ridge, against heavy enemy opposition. After a short spell of relief August 25th found them attacking and pushing well forward to the east of the Carnoy to Suzanne Road. At the end of the day his battalion was lying astride the Fricourt –Maricourt Road, east of Carnoy after capturing Carre Wood and an elaborate trench system.

Maricourt village was attacked by them on 27th and the next day his battalion captured German positions between Bois d'Haut and Support Copse. It would have been in one of these battles that he was wounded and moved back to the Rouen area where there were many military hospitals for the seriously wounded.

Pte. Alfred Monk Herts Express September 21st 1918

His mother sadly received conflicting communications around the time of his injury that gave her hope, including one from her son saying that he had been wounded but hoped to get home.

Pte. **Alfred Monk** died, aged 20 in No. 12 General Hospital, Rouen and was buried at the St Sever Extension Cemetery, area 9, plot II, row O, grave 4.

Ernest Arthur Morgan

Date of Birth: 27-5-1892
First School: Hitchin British Infants' School
Hitchin Boys' British School
Date of Admission: 29-5-1899
Parents: Henry (Harry) and Emma
Address on admission: Charlton
Left school: 25-5-1906
Occupation: Butcher's boy

Ernest's medals

1901 Census details

The family was living in Charlton village, on the outskirts of Hitchin. Father Harry 32, was a brewer's drayman. His wife Emily 32, had William 11 and **Ernest Arthur** 9, to look after. She was born in Willian but the others were born in Charlton.

1911 Census details

Harry, aged 42 was now a mineral water maker in a hotel. The boys, at 21 and 18 were both butchers' salesmen.

Military details

Ernest enlisted in Hitchin in 1914 but there are no service records remaining. He was Private G/2680 in the 9th Battalion East Surrey Regiment. His medal entitlement details show him as going over to the front on October 5th 1915, so in fact he survived for less than 5 weeks!

His regiment was part of the 72nd Brigade, 24th Infantry Division and there is no divisional history to help us. The division had been at Loos in September 1915 and had gone up to the Ypres area from there.

Pte. **Ernest Morgan** was recorded as dying from wounds received on November 10th 1915, although there were no major battles at that time. He was 23.

He is buried at the Reninghelst New Military Cemetery, Poperinghe near Ypres, Belgium, plot 1, row B, grave 2. When I visited on a damp autumn day I found that the family had had the moving words 'Peace Perfect Peace, God is Love' put at the base of his headstone.

His family's inscription

Ernest Odell

Date of Birth: 28-6-1879
First School: Hitchin British Infants' School
Hitchin Boys' British School
Date of Admission: 21-6-1886
Parents: Robert (a dealer) and Esther
Address on admission: Russell's Slip
Left school: 16-7-1891   Occupation: ?

The name Odell has caused me some confusion as on some official documents it appears as O'Dell and on others Odell. I have had to make a decision and looked at Robert's own signature on the 1911 census and went by that, no apostrophe!

1881 Census details

The family was living at Parcel's Yard. Robert was 38 and a general dealer. All the family was born in Hitchin. Esther was 41 and their children were Thomas 4 and **Ernest** 2.

1891 Census details

The family was living at 3, Sharp's Yard where Robert was 48 and his wife 51. They had **Ernest** 12, Nellie 10, George 4 and Jack 3, living with them.

1901 Census details

Ernest, a gardener who was now said to be 21, was the head of the household with Nellie, George and Jack with him. They were living at 10 Russells' Slip. It appears that Robert and Esther died in 1897 and 1899.

Ernest married Alice Louisa French in the summer of 1907.

1911 Census details

Ernest is now recorded as 34 and Alice 26. They were living at 7 Taylor's Cottages.

They had Emily Odell 3 and little Alice French 6, with them.

Military details

There is a problem here. The Commonwealth War Graves certificate on his death in January 1919 confirms him as the son of Robert and husband of Alice Louisa but suggests he was first 4622 in the 4th Battalion Essex Regiment but his medal index card shows him as 35512 in the Essex Regiment before transfer to the 47th P.O.W. Labour Company, Labour Corps (604768).

Until mid 1916, German prisoners were sent to England. From this time onward, prisoners were initially sent to Abbeville. Men with useful skills, notably forestry and engineering, were drafted into companies of about 100 men each, for use in POW Forestry Companies and Army Service Corps and Royal Engineers workshops respectively. 47 such POW labour companies were attached to the Labour Corps when it was formed.

His medal entitlement shows that he did not see service until 1916. The fact that he died at home means that he could have been

Ernest's grave

injured and sent home. As there are no service or pension records surviving it is impossible to conclude what service and in which theatre he was involved but his time was certainly spent abroad as he had campaign medals.

He died on January 24th 1919 aged 39 and is buried in Hitchin Cemetery, N.E. Extension, grave 635. 'Rest In Peace' is inscribed at the base of the headstone.

Richard Martin Odell

Date of Birth: 21-6-1889
First School: Hitchin British Infants' School
Hitchin Boys' British School
Date of Admission: 24-5-1897
Parents: Stephen (a blacksmith) and Elizabeth
Address on admission: 60 Hitchin Hill
Left school: ?   Occupation: ?

1891 Census details

The family was living at 8 Kent Place. Stephen, a farrier was 40, his wife Bessie (née Martin), was 37 and they had Lily 10, Jennie 9, Bob 6, Elizabeth 5 and **Dick**, 2.

1901 Census details

They were living at 60 Hitchin Hill and they had new additions, Beatrice 10 and Leonard 9.

1911 Census and Military details

Richard was now registered on the census as a Stoker in the navy at the Royal Naval Barracks, Chatham, aged 22.

Sadly Stoker **Richard Odell** died aged 25 on January 1st 1915 when his ship H.M.S. Formidable was torpedoed by German submarine U-24 off Portland Bill in Dorset as was described below on the HMS Formidable website.

'The squadron was participating in gunnery exercises off Portland, supported by the cruisers Topaz and Diamond. On the night of 31 December after the exercises, the fleet remained at sea even though submarine activity had been reported in the area. With the wind increasing and rough sea conditions, submarine attacks would have been difficult to carry out effectively and so were not thought to be a significant threat. The next day, H.M.S. Formidable was steaming at 10 knots at the rear of the squadron just 20 miles from Star Point, when at 02:20 she was struck by a torpedo on the starboard

side giving her a list of 20 degrees. 45 minutes later she was struck by a second torpedo. The launch along with two other boats (one of which capsized soon after) was launched, and the two light cruisers managed to pick up 80 men. H.M.S. Formidable remained afloat until 04:45, and then went down quickly with Captain Arthur Noel Loxley still on the bridge along with his Fox Terrier Bruce. In rough seas near Berry Head, a Brixham trawler, the Provident under the command of Captain W. Piller, picked up the men from the launch before it sank, saving 71 members of the crew. The second pinnace took off another 70 men. This boat was spotted from the shore the following night and a further 48 men were brought ashore alive 22 hours after the sinking.

The total loss of life on Formidable was 35 Officers and 512 men out of 780.

The wreck site is designated and controlled under the Protection of Military Remains Act. Captain Loxley's dog, Bruce, was washed ashore and is buried in a marked grave in Abbotsbury Gardens in Dorset.'

Stoker Odell's name appears on the Chatham Memorial to the Missing and his mother would have later received the 1914 Star as well as the War and Victory medals. His father had died in the second quarter of 1916.

HMS Formidable

Archibald Bernard Orsman

Date of Birth: 22-5-1895
First School: St Saviour's
Hitchin Boys' British School
Date of Admission: 4-5-1903
Parents: Arthur (a carpenter) and Eleanor
Address on admission: 9 Verulam Road
Left school: 11-6-1909   Occupation: Errand boy

1901 Census details

At the Verulam Road address, father Arthur 49, and Eleanor 47, had Francis 19, a cabinet maker, Reginald 17, a baker's boy, Victor 9, Stanley 7, **Archie** 5 and Hilda 5. (twins?)

1911 Census details

Still at the same address, the parents declared that they had been married for 30 years and had 8 living children. **Archie** was an errand boy in a boot shop.

Military Details

He enlisted in Bedford and became G/26406 in the 17th Battalion Duke of Cambridge's Own (Middlesex) Regiment. The 2 medals awarded indicate that he went over to France after the beginning of 1916. No service or pension records have survived. A newspaper report showed that he worked for a boot repairer in the Church Yard before joining up in April 1915.

On the 28th & 29th April 1917 he was involved in the Battle of Arras. On the 28th his battalion which was also known as "The 1st Football Battalion" (was he a sportsman at school ?) lined up in front of Oppy Wood and Oppy village (6th Brigade, 2nd Infantry Division) and attacked. There were heavy losses. The Germans held the wood and the village in strength. His parents did not receive news of his demise and in the June newspaper he was recorded as missing. Added to their concern was the fact that their two other sons were in action, Stanley in France and Frank in Salonika.

Middlesex Regiment badge

Pte. **Archibald Orsman** was actually killed in action, aged 21, on April 28th and his name appears on Bay 7 of the Arras Memorial to the Missing.

Faubourg D'Amiens Cemetery, Arras

Walter Charles Pearce

Date of Birth: 12-10-1880
First School: ?
Hitchin Boys' British School
Date of Admission: 6-6-1887
Parents: John and Ann
Address on admission: Foundry Road [Bedford Street]
Left school: 1894   Occupation: ?

1881 Census details

The family was living at Duckland's Farm. Father John 25, was an agricultural labourer and his wife Ann was a 26 year old straw plaiter. They had Gertrude 4, Sarah 2 and **Walter Charles** 5 months.

1891 Census details

The family was now living at 59 Old Park Road. where **Walter,** now 10 was recorded as a scholar and sisters Kate 8 and Ellen 4 had arrived.

1901 Census details

Walter was now a domestic gardener, living as a boarder at an address in Welwyn, with a 76 year old widow.

1911 Census details

Walter 30, was now recorded as a boarder with the Parfitt family at 78 Church Street, Chelsea and was working as a nurseryman.

Military details

Some of **Walter's** service records have survived so we can conclude a few details.

☆ He enlisted in Hitchin November 29th 1915 and was medically examined in Bedford.

☆ He joined the 4th Battalion, Bedfordshire Regiment as No. 23634.

☆ He was 5 feet 7 ½ inches in height with a chest expansion of 37 ½ inches.

☆ He trained from November 29th 1915 to July 9th 1916 (294 days) and went over to France on July 10th 1916 (7 days into the Somme Offensive). His battalion along with others was put into the 190th Brigade of the 63rd (Royal Naval) Division.

He would have been involved in the Operations on the Ancre in November 1916 and in early 1917 in the actions around the area of Miraumont.

During the battle of Arras, they were heavily involved in the second battle of the Scarpe when they took Gavrelle and the action at Arleux in April.

On April 28th they received sudden orders to prepare for battle again and went to the assembly trenches in order to attack Oppy Trench the following day.

On 29th they attacked and captured it but were counter attacked. They finally re-captured the objective at 11 am. They were heavily shelled all day before being relieved by the Honourable Artillery Company. Many casualties were recorded that day and Walter was one, for, as the service records state, he received gun-shot wounds to the spine that paralysed him. Little did he know that another past pupil of his school, Archibald Orsman was fighting in the same battle and was killed on 28th.

Headstone for Walter in Hitchin cemetery

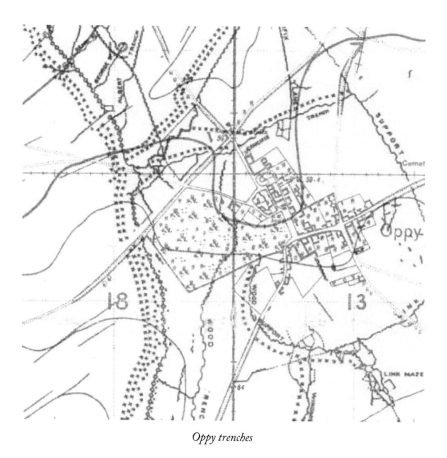

Oppy trenches

Pte. **Walter Pearce** was transferred back to England where reports were made at the King George Hospital, London declaring him to be unfit for service and indeed work. Thus a pension was calculated based on 1 year, 203 days of service. Sadly as a result of his dreadful injuries he died, aged 37 on November 21st 1917 and is buried in Hitchin Cemetery, S.E. Extension, grave 756.

Arthur John Pilsworth

Date of Birth: 11-10-1888
First School: St Philip's Cambridge
Hitchin Boys' British School

Date of Admission: 15-5-1899
Parents: John (an engine driver) and Mary A
Address on admission: Florence Street
Left school: 31-1-1902   Occupation: Grocer's boy

1901 Census details

The family was living at 51 Florence Street having moved from Cambridge. Father John 35, was an engine driver. His wife Mary A. was 34, (she died in 1934) and they had 6 children. Harry was 14 and a sewing machine maker, **Arthur John** was 12, George was 11, Ernest was 5, Sidney was 3 and there was an infant under 1 month who they later named John.

1911 Census details

Still in Florence Street Father and 2 sons, Harry and George were working for the railways, Ernest was an assistant house painter, aged 14, Sidney was 12, John 10 and Mary had new daughter, Alice 7.

Arthur John had left home and from a report in the Hertfordshire Express of September 14th 1918 we know that he had been apprenticed in the International Stores in the Market Place, then went to Nottingham to work in a branch there. He married and had twins, a boy and a girl but his wife died about 1913 and so the children were left in the care of their grandmother Mary in Hitchin and he went as a manager to a branch of the Home and Colonial Stores in Leicestershire. This is where he met his second wife, Elizabeth Warner. They married at St Saviour's in Leicester on August 2nd 1917. This story took a great deal of investigation but the Leicester marriage certificate proved it all!

Military details

Arthur enlisted at the beginning of 1918 in Hinckley, Leicestershire as Guardsman 4178 in the 1st Battalion Welsh Guards.

On August 25th 1918 the 3rd Guards Brigade attempted to make a fresh attempt to reach Ecoust and Longatte in France and in so doing capture the German held reserve trenches on the way. They set off from between St Leger Woods and the village of Croisilles. Even though they were assisted by tanks, the 2nd Battalion Scots Guards and the 1st Battalion Grenadier Guards they could make no progress, all suffering severely from the incessant machine- gun fire from both the front and flanks. Sadly they had to withdraw.

The 1st Battalion Welsh Guards, north of St Leger were held up by uncut enemy barbed wire defences and came under heavy machine-gun fire from three sides and they too were eventually driven back with heavy losses. Later the 3rd

ORPHAN TWINS.

SAD WALSWORTH BEREAVEMENT.

A sad war bereavement is involved in the latest casualty from Walsworth, in which Pte. Arthur John Pilsworth (31), Welsh Guards, son of Mrs. Pilsworth, widow, Walsworth, was killed, the date being August 25. The late Pte. Pilsworth leaves two children (twins) by his first wife, a boy and a girl, who came to live with their grandmother when their mother died about 5 years ago. He was apprenticed at the International Stores at Hitchin, and after being employed in one of the branch shops at Nottingham went as manager of one of the Home and Colonial Stores in Leicestershire. He entered the Army about eight months ago, and had been in France about eleven weeks. Mrs. Pilsworth has a son, Ernest William, now in hospital at Cambridge with illness, having served nearly three years in the Army, during which he was wounded by gun-shot in both legs, and also gassed. Her youngest son, Sidney, aged 19, is now in France.

THREE HITCHIN

The sad newspaper report

Guards Brigade received a letter from the Divisional Commander saying how much he appreciated the difficulty of the task they had been set and that he " knew that they had done all that was humanly possible".

Guardsman **Arthur Pilsworth** aged 29 was killed on August 25th 1918, after only 11 weeks in that action and is buried in Bucquoy Road Cemetery, Ficheux, France in plot VII, row B, grave 23. How sad that he had left behind a new wife of one year and a mother who was caring for his two small children from his first marriage. At the base of his headstone is inscribed 'Though Distance Divides Fond Memories Cling'. I found the visit to this cemetery particularly moving. I had 2 graves to visit, **Arthur's** and one other personal one. They both made me very emotional because of all the detective work involved. I resolved to complete their stories and ensure that they would be visited and not forgotten.

A moving tribute

The second grave was that of Pte. Ephraim Wilson M.M. whose Memorial Plaque I had bought at auction in 2011. This young man had been born in Ashdon near Saffron Walden and had emigrated to Winnipeg in Canada where my only brother lives. Ephraim came to Europe with the Canadian Infantry and was awarded the Military Medal. I did a tremendous amount of research into his family and military story, then, by pure coincidence discovered his medals were being sold by a Calgary medals dealer. So my heart ruled my head and we purchased his medals,

Ephraim's memorial plaque

which I have proudly re-united with his Memorial Plaque, or as they are often called, the 'Death Penny'.

Interestingly, buried in that same cemetery alongside his Canadian comrades is Private Joseph Standing Buffalo who was killed aged 20, on 29th September 1918. He was the son of Julius Standing Buffalo of the Sioux Tribe of Fort Qu'Appelle, Saskatchewan, Canada and the grandson of Chief Sitting Bull, who together with Chief Crazy Horse, led the Sioux as they attacked and massacred the troops led by General Custer at the Battle of Little Big Horn in 1876.

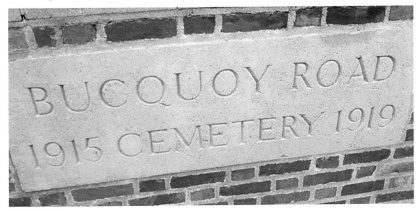

Bucquoy Road Cemetery

Frederick John Read

Date of Birth: 24-5-1889
First School: Sunnyside

Hitchin Boys' British School
Date of Admission: 7-9-1896
Parents: George, (a brick maker) and Emma
Address on admission: Black Horse Lane
Left school: 23-1-1903   Occupation: Carpenter

1891 Census details

The family was living at Brick Kiln, Bedford Road. where George 47, (born in Bedford) and Emma 40, (born in Preston) had 4 children. William was 24 and employed as a printer, Annie was 15, May 3 and **Frederick** was 2.

1901 Census details

They were living at Black Horse Lane and by now had the following children living at home, Edith, 13 (who I think was May from the 1881 census) **Frederick** 11, Florence 9, Clara 8 and Rose 6, who were all born in Hitchin.

1911 Census details

George was 67 and still working and Emma was 60. They stated that they had been married for 25 years and had had 6 children with 5 still living, but 7 had been listed earlier! They had 4 rooms in their home at 6 Black Horse Lane. **Frederick** now 21, was a house painter and Rose Gertrude was 16. Those two were still at home.

Military Details

Frederick was working as an estate painter on the King's Walden Bury estate in 1914. The 290 acre estate was owned by Thomas Fenwick Harrison and by 1916 the house was used as a convalescent home for wounded soldiers .**Frederick** enlisted in September 1914 in Hitchin soon after getting married to Agnes and having a child. After training in Shoreham he went over to the Front in August 1915. We know that he qualified for 3 medals (Qualifying date August 30th 1915) although no service or pension records have survived. He was Private 16339 in the 8th Battalion Bedfordshire Regiment. For most of their service the 8th was with the 16th Brigade, 6th Division. **Private Read** came home on leave in February 1916 and when he returned to his unit it was near Ypres in Belgium. He sadly died on Good Friday (April 21st) A later newspaper report states that he had posted a postcard on that day saying he was all right but subsequently a shell burst over his trench with fatal consequences.

The Divisional history tells of his battalion being involved in minor operations near Turco Farm and the nearby Morteldje Estaminet on 19th-22nd April 1916.

As his name is on the Menin Gate Memorial to the Missing in Ypres, Panels 31-33, we must assume that he is one of those missing and still lying in the now peaceful and tranquil fields of the area. He was 26.

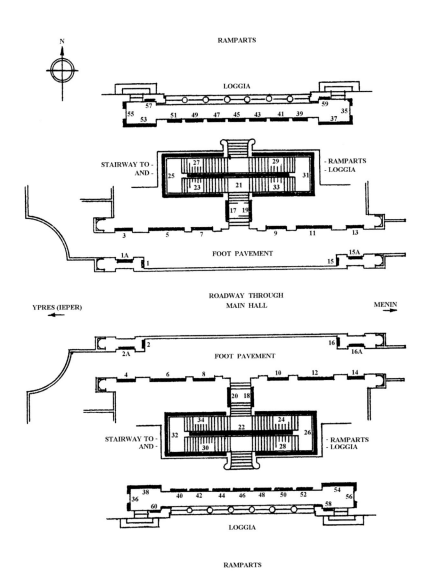

LAYOUT OF THE YPRES (MENIN GATE) MEMORIAL PANELS

Menin Gate plan

Raymond Robinson (cousin of Harold Barker)

Date of Birth: 12-4-1896
First School: St Saviour's Infant
Hitchin Boys' British School
Date of Admission: 1-5-1903
Parents: William, (a gardener) and Hephzibah
Address on admission: 19, Benslow Lane
Left school: 4-5-1910 Occupation: Builder's clerk

1901 Census details

The family was living at 19 Benslow Lane. Father William 38, (born in Royston) was a gardener. His wife Hephzibah 38, (born in Barley) had 4 children to care for, Alfred 7, William C. 6, **Raymond C.** 4 and Stella M. 10 months. They were all born in Hitchin.

1911 Census details

The 3 older children were now occupied locally. Alfred 17, was a baker's assistant, William 16, was an electrician's assistant and **Raymond** 14, was a clerk at the joinery works of Messrs. P.H. Barker at 86, Bancroft, whilst Stella 10 was still at school.

William and Hepsy had been married for 18 years and the family was recorded as having 4 rooms in their home at 19 Benslow Lane.

Name.	Corps.	Rank.	Regtl. No.
ROBINSON	2/2 Coy Suss: R.G.A	A/Cpl:	374449
Raymond Cecil	270 S B R G A	2/Lieut ✕	
	Appt: Comm: 2/Lt: R.G.A. 4 2/18		

Medal.	Roll.	Page.	Remarks.
RGA -VICTORY -✕-	Off. 139.	249E	IVX/107.Off. 10/5/22 NW/7/15513. Died 19/10/18
BRITISH	"		
STAR			

Theatre of War first served in: France
Date of entry therein: —

23/2/22 NW/7/15513 K. 1380

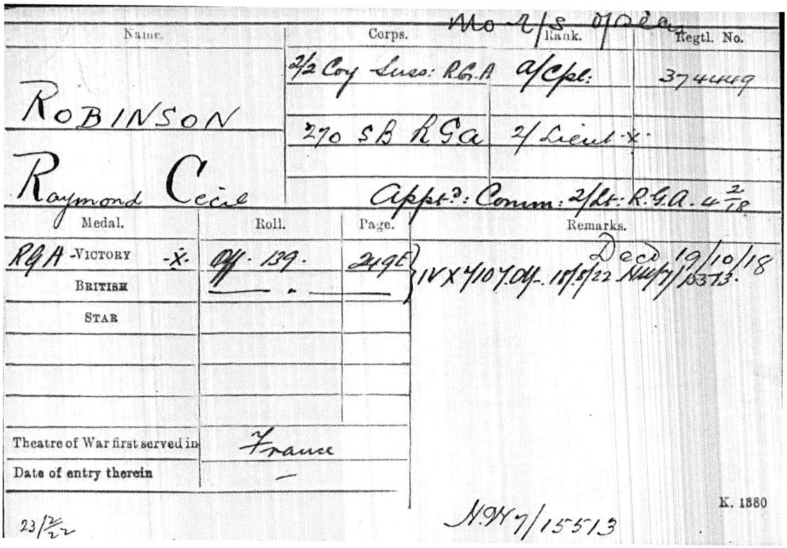

Medals entitlement

Military details

He enlisted in 1915 and from his medals entitlement it can be concluded that he went over to France after the beginning of 1916 as he had 2 medals, the War and Victory medals. The newspaper report suggests that it was April 1917.

According to the medal entitlement card he was in 2/2 Company Suss. (Sussex?) R.G.A. (374449) as Acting Corporal then later, on April 4th 1918 he is recorded as 2nd Lieut. in the 270th Siege Battery R.G.A.

Our soldier's siege battery was involved in the final push in October, with the enemy retreating back to the Hindenberg Line and 2nd Lt. **Raymond Robinson,** aged 22, died from wounds received in action on October 19th so close to the end of hostilities. He is buried in Vadencourt British Military Cemetery, Maissemy, Aisne, France. plot 11, row C, grave 27 where I visited him to pay my respects.

Newspaper report.

Saturday November 2nd 1918
Hitchin Officer Killed
Promoted from the ranks
Great sorrow is felt from the death from wounds received in action in France on October 19th of 2nd-Lieut Raymond Cecil Robinson RGA third son of Mr and Mrs William Robinson of Benslow Lane Hitchin. The deceased was well known in the town being on the office staff of Messrs P.H. Barker and Son, Hitchin. His efficiency and smartness quickly bought him promotion from the ranks. He joined up about 3 years ago and went to France last April, taking part in the victorious actions since then. Lieut. Robinson was 22 years of age last April. Many expressions of sympathy have been received by the bereaved family. Mr and Mrs Robinson have two other sons in France.

The R.G.A. in action

George Ryall

Date of Birth: 17-9-1900
First School: Newport Pagnell
Hitchin Boys' British School
Date of Admission: 10-3-1908
Parents: Arthur (a parchment maker) and Florence
Address on admission: 48 Bunyan Road
Left school: ?   Occupation: ?

1901 Census details.

Mother Florence 27, (née Pratt), was living with her parents at 50 Mill Road, Leighton Buzzard, where she and her father were born. Her father William Pratt 52, was a house painter and mother Julia 53, was born in Devon. Florence's siblings were Kate 17 and William E. 14. Florence has 6 month old little **George** with her but husband Arthur was boarding with Alfred and Florence Davies (38 and 31) at 208 Albany Road, Camberwell, where he was a parchment maker.

1911 Census details

Arthur 33, was still working as a parchment maker and had been married to Florence 37, for 12 years. They were living at 48 Bunyan Road, with their 4 children, **George** 10 (born in Potton), Doris 8 and Albert 6, (who were born in Brentford) and Kathleen 1, (who was born in Hitchin).

Military details

George enlisted with his close friend Harold Barker. They signed up on October 23rd 1918 into the Queen's Royal West Surrey Regiment and George's regimental number was TR 161742. They were both in training at St Albans when the dreaded Spanish Flu hit the pair and they sadly died within a day of each other at the St Albans Military Hospital.

He is buried in Hitchin Cemetery, N.E. area, grave 606 with the touching inscription that his family would have paid for, 'Underneath Are The Everlasting Arms'.

An extract from a newspaper article published on Saturday November 16th 1918.

In death undivided
The influenza scourge has claimed as two of its' victims, Pte Harold Barker, eldest son of Mr and Mrs Barker of 2 Cambridge Terrace, Nightingale Road, (whose death was announced last week) and Pte George Ryall, eldest son of Mr and Mrs Arthur Ryall of Bunyan Road. It is a sad coincidence that both victims were only eighteen years of age, both enlisted in the Queens R.W. Surreys on October 23rd and both were stationed at St Albans where both passed away within a day of each other.

Pte Barker died from pneumonia following influenza on Monday November 4th and Pte Ryall died the next day at 7.50am.

The two boys had been closely connected, they had attended school together, joined the boy scouts together and entered Messrs Russells employment together. At a later stage Pte Barker went on to work for Messrs P.H. Barker and Son, (joinery works) at 86 Bancroft.

The two deceased soldiers enlisted with another Hitchin youth named Appleby and the three were deeply attached. A close comradeship and an affectionate friendship has thus been ruthlessly shattered by the universal scourge.

George's Grave

Alfred James Sapsed

Date of Birth: 11-11-1894
First School: Royston
Hitchin Boys' British School
Date of Admission: 4-3-1907
Parents: James (a farm worker) and Mary
Address on admission: Grove Mill Farm
Left school: ?   Occupation: ?

1881 Census details

Father (to be) James 16, was living in Barkway near Royston with the Stoten family and was recorded as the nephew. He was an agricultural labourer.

James married Mary in 1889 but the family seems to have slipped through the census net as they can't be found anywhere until 1911.

1911 Census details

James 45, (born in Royston) was a horseman on a farm and had been married for 22 years to Mary 46, (born in Shepreth, north of Royston). They had had 9 children of whom 8 were still living and at home. George 21, was a groom, **Alfred** 16, was a laundry van boy at the Pioneer Laundry in Letchworth, Arthur was 13, Charles was 11, Ernest was 7, Herbert was 5 and Grace was 2. She was born in Hitchin but the other children's births were registered in Royston. The family was living in a 6 roomed home in Walsworth.

Military details

No service or pension records remain for Alfred but he was awarded 3 medals so we know that he joined the 6th Battalion Bedfordshire Regiment (12069) in or before 1915 and was trained and over in France by July 3rd. He went to France in July 1915 with Stanley Herbert Leete from whom he took over distribution of the Hitchin War Comforts Fund (according to David Baines). I have four sets of the Leete brothers' medals. The 6th Beds were part of the 112th Brigade, 37th Division. The war diary shows that they had a dreadful year in 1916 in 4 major battles.

Newspaper obituary

By the time of his death at only 22 he had been promoted to Sergeant. The Bedfordshires were involved in the Battle of Arras, which started in a snowstorm on April 9th 1917 and by the time it ended in mid-May, the total losses were over 159,000.

Arras Memorial, Bay 5

The village of Monchy le Preux, held by the Germans, was on top of high ground overlooking a very large part of the area near Arras and was a very important part of their highly defended and fortified Hindenburg Line. Our attack on the village, 9-12th April, cost Sgt. **Alfred Sapsed** his life and those of many, many more. Although the division was relieved on the night of the 12th, it was too late for our soldier. He was not found hence his name is on Bay 5 of the Arras Memorial to the Missing.

James Henry Sewell

Date of Birth: 13-6-1896
First School: St Saviour's Infant
Hitchin Boys' British School
Date of Admission: 7-9-1903
Parents: James (a carpenter GNR) and Emma Elizabeth
Address on admission: 50 Radcliffe Road
Left school: 10-6-1910
Occupation: Before enlisting he was employed by Messrs. Spencer & Co. Engineering Works

1901 Census details

Despite much searching no record can be found of the family in this census. My feeling is, that James (senior) could have been married before.

1911 Census details

This reveals that James, now 64 and Emma 52, had been married for only 16 years and had 14 year old **James Henry**. They were living at 50 Radcliffe Road with 2 lodgers. They only had the one child and would have been 48 and 36 when they married.

From newspaper reports of the time we know that **James** (junior) was earlier a member of the Church Lads' Brigade and worked for Spencer and Co. Engineering Works, Walsworth, after leaving school.

Military details

He joined up with his friend from school, George Farrow on January 6th 1914. **James** went into the 1st Hertfordshire Regiment (2133) then is recorded as 265385 in the Beds and Herts on his medal entitlement card. He was in the first period of training when war broke out and after that went over to France in July 1915, aged 19. He was wounded 12 months later (His service records show this as gun shot wounds on July 8th 1916) but he returned to the trenches in January 1917. By this time he is recorded as Lance Corporal then Corporal before reverting to Private. Yet the C.W.G.C. states that he died as a Corporal.

He qualified for the 3 medals and was sadly killed aged 21 on the first day of the dreadful battle of Passchendaele on July 31st 1917.

The 1st Battalion. Hertfordshire Regiment was part of the 118th Brigade, 39th Division.

In **1915** the battalion was engaged during the winter actions at Cuinchy in February, the Battle of Festubert in May and at the Battle of Loos in September.

In **1916** the battalion was engaged in the Battles of the Somme, including being lightly involved in the Battle of the Ancre Heights in October, as well as in the Battle of the Ancre in November.

In **1917** the battalion was heavily engaged during the opening day of the Battles of Ypres (also called the Third Battle of Ypres and Passchendaele), when the battalion lost over 450 men during their assault on St Julien, part of the Battle of Pilkem. On that dreadful day they were attacking towards St Julien, north west of Ypres. The Hertfordshires were cut down by the German machine gun

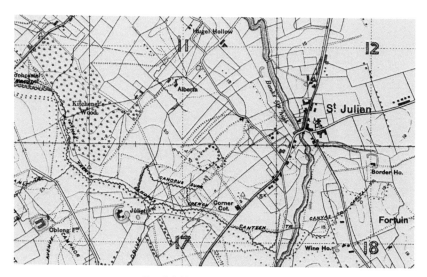

Battlefield at St Julien, Belgium

fire as they advanced and later, the survivors, suffering from heavy enemy counter attacks were forced to withdraw from that village to the banks of the small river called the Steenbeek.

Cpl. **James Sewell** was never found hence his name being among those recorded on the Menin Gate Memorial to the Missing in Ypres Panels 54-56. He was 21.

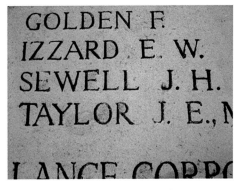

Menin Gate Memorial

Ernest William Smith

Date of Birth: 12-4-1885
First School: St Saviour's Infant
Hitchin Boys' British School
Date of Admission: 19-6-1893
Parents: William (a shunter GNR) and Mary
Address on admission: 52 Dacre Road
Left school: 14-5-1898   Occupation: ?

Duke of Wellington's West Riding Regiment Badge

1891 Census details

The family was living at 52 Dacre Road and William (born Bocking, Essex), was 38 and a shunter with GNR. His wife Mary 37, was caring for their 5 children, Bertram 10, (born Islington) Lillian 7, (born in Bocking), **Ernest 5,** Sidney 3, (both born in Hitchin) and Gertrude 4 months, (also born in Bocking).

1901 Census details

Recorded at the same address in Dacre Road. the family had dispersed as Bertram and **Ernest** were living elsewhere but the other children were at home.

1911 Census details

Father William now 59 and Mary 57 had Lillian 28 and Sidney 23, still living at home at the same address. Little did they know that between then and 1918 they were to lose one son in the service of his country and Lillian and Sidney were to move to Canada, where Bertram had already moved, as researched from the service records of **Ernest** which have largely survived.

Ernest (26), a railway passenger guard for GNR was now married (at St Michael's Church, Wood Green on March 21st 1909) to Mary Catherine, 28 (née Nash) and living at 52 Westfield Road, Hornsey, London with their child Lillian Maud 1, (born August 11th 1911 at 17 Brabant Road, Wood Green) and Mother–in-law, Elizabeth Nash, a 'monthly nurse'.

Military details

Ernest enlisted at Wood Green on June 6th 1916, as 60033 in the Queen's (Royal West Surrey) Regiment and after training, went over to France on June 6th 1917.

☆ According to the service records, 41 pages of which survived;
☆ He was 5 feet 5 inches tall with a chest measurement of 36 ¾ inches when fully expanded.
☆ He weighed 130lbs.
☆ He was transferred into the Duke of Wellington's (West Riding) Regiment as 33635 on January 29th 1918 and posted March 20th 1918.
☆ He was reported as wounded and missing on July 21st 1918.

In July 1918, his battalion as part of the 186th Brigade, 62nd (2nd West Riding) Division had been seconded, together with other British divisions, to assist the French armies which were under a heavy German attack on the River Ardre, as the Germans attempted to drive through to Paris. This was known as the Battle of Tardenois.

On July 20th-21st, he and his comrades were fighting in the area of Marfaux on that river and it was very hard going.

Ernest was posted as missing but in fact he had been captured and taken to Germany as a P.O.W. He was repatriated at the end of the war and on December 6th 1918 was at the West Riding Division Depot and became ill so he was taken to No. 2. Scottish Hospital, Edinburgh arriving there on Dec. 7th.

Ernest was buried in the family grave in Hitchin

115

Despite being treated, he died on 31st from acute nephritis, (kidney problems and failure) aged 33. The medical report shows that the nephritis was caused by exposure whilst on active service.

Sgt. **Ernest Smith's** body was claimed by his wife and taken south for burial at Hitchin Cemetery N.E.628. From July 7th 1919 she received a pension of 20 shillings and 5 pence per week for herself and her one child Lillian Maud.

The service records show a poignant finale as on May 19th 1919 his personal effects were returned to Mary and listed as:
Hairbrush, toothbrush, two combs, shaving brush, mirror, razor in case, holdall, toothpaste and a pencil.
She then acknowledged receipt of this pitiful little bundle on May 27th.

Samuel Smith

Date of Birth: 3-5-1891
First School: Hitchin British Infants' School
Hitchin Boys' British School
Date of Admission: 29-5-1899
Parents: James (labourer on local roads but died between 1897 and 1901) and Martha
Address on admission: Adam and Eve Alley
Left school: 25-5-1906
Occupation: Tanyard boy (at Fellmongers)

The Royal Berkshire Regiment cap badge

1891 Census details

The family was living at 6 Adam and Eve Alley. James 45 was a labourer, (born Silsoe, Beds.) and Martha (or Mary) 43, was a laundress. The children were Rhoda E. 14, James 11, Emma 9, Mary A. 6 and John 3. **Samuel** arrived a month later. Mother and children were all born in Hitchin.

1901 census details

Widowed Martha, 53 was a charwoman. Some children had left home but Emma 19 and Mary A 17, were straw plaiters working at home. John was 13, **Samuel** 10 and James 4.

1911 Census details

Only 3 children were now living at home with Martha 63; John aged 23, was a bricklayer's labourer, **Samuel** 20, a general labourer and Mary Ann, 25 was still plaiting straw for the local hat making industry.

Military details

Samuel was married to Edith and working for G.W. Russell and Son, (leather dressers/fellmongers), Bancroft when he enlisted to fight for his country. He was first in the Hertfordshire Yeomanry (105985) before being transferred into the 1st Battalion, Royal Berkshire Regiment as 220722.

From his medals entitlement we know that he went across to the battlefield after the beginning of 1916.

During 1916 his 2nd Division was in action at the Somme from July to November and in 1917 was involved in several areas of conflict so **Samuel** had a traumatic time.

In 1918 the battalion had been withdrawn from the fighting areas and was in fact 'at rest' when he was killed on June 1st but from the Hitchin newspaper report of June 22nd it transpires that he was killed alongside 3 others when an enemy shell hit their billets.

The sad information was relayed to the young widow Edith, living in Charlton, by his C.O. and the mother of another Hitchin lad who was serving in the same regiment. His C.O. said that he was one of the best of men, respected by all who knew him and always cheerful in his work and ready to volunteer. Edith re-married a Mr. Walker.

Pte. **Samuel Smith** who was only 27, is buried in the Warlincourt Halte British Cemetery at Saulty, in plot XI, row C, grave 17.

Walter Smith

Date of Birth: 17-12-1882
First School: Beechwood Board School, Leighton [Essex?]
Hitchin Boys' British School
Date of admission 13-3-1893
Parents: Archelaus W (a police constable) and Emma
Address on admission: Old Park Road
Left school: 11-4-1896   Occupation: ?

1881 Census details

The family was living at Musley Hill, Ware. Archelaus (born in Kings Walden) was 36 and a police constable and Emma his wife, (born in Charlton, Hitchin) was 33. They had George 10, (born in Hitchin) and Frances W. 5, Annie 2 and Flora 7 months, all born in Ware.

1891 Census details

They were now living at Flamstead and 10 years on, Archelaus was still in the police. George did not appear on the census having probably left home but they now had young **Walter** 8, who had been born in Sandon, near Buntingford and Lillie 5, Harry 2 and Percy 9 months, who were all born in Flamstead.

1901 Census details

They were now living at 4, Hope Cottages, Old Park Road and Archelaus had retired. Only Lillie, Harry and Percy were still at home with their parents and **Walter** could not be found anywhere until he turned up in 1911.

1911 Census details

Archelaus had died and widow Emma 63 was alone with Percy, now a house painter. She had been married for 43 years and had had 11 children of whom 10 were still living. 4 Hope Cottages had, according to the census, 6 rooms. **Walter**, now 28 and still single was a boarder living with widow Lucy Andrew and her family at 5 Andover Street, Sheffield. He had also become a policeman and had a colleague lodging with him.

Military details

Walter enlisted in Hitchin at the beginning of the war as he qualified for the 1914 Star, plus the War and Victory medals and went out to France on November 8th 1914. He was said to be residing in Hitchin at the time. He was put into the 2nd Bedfordshire Regiment, which became at first, part of the 21st Brigade in the 7th Division then transferred to the 89th Brigade, 30th Division. It was said that there was a chronic shortage of equipment to train with!

During early 1916 the battalion was in trenches around Maricourt, south east of Albert where the terrible weather caused almost as much hardship as the enemy fire.

In March, the war diary of the battalion notes that there were very quiet days with again more snow. Only a few men were lost due to shelling or sickness. Then on March 14th they experienced heavy enemy shelling in Maricourt at 9.50 pm when the diary records *'2 O.R. killed, 1 wounded'*.

Our **Sergeant Walter Smith** was one of the O.R. or 'other ranks' sadly killed on that day. He was 33. His company were either at West Keep, Mound Keep or on the Peronne Road.

1914 Star Trio

Every cemetery entrance has a register available

It seems that he was buried at that time but that he was re-located to Cerisy-Gailly Military Cemetery, about 4 miles away from Maricourt behind the line sometime later when much consolidating took place. He lies there in plot II, row D, grave 13 alongside over 600 others.

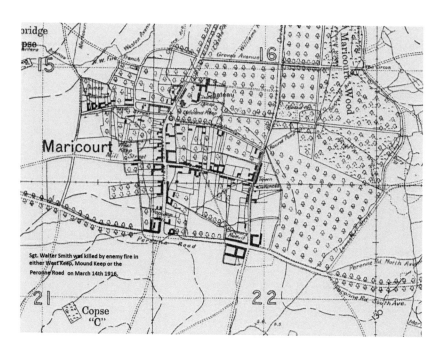

Sgt. Walter Smith was killed by enemy fire in either West Keep, Mound Keep or the Peronne Road on March 14th 1916.

Sgt. Walter Smith was killed near Maricourt

Frederick Waldron Stimpson

Date of Birth: 5-2-1879
First School: Hitchin British Infants' School
Hitchin Boys' British School
Date of admission 21-9-1885 to 17-1-1889 and re-admitted 11-3-1889
Parents: Richard (died between 1881 and 1885) and Sarah
Address on admission: Back Street
Left school: 13-9-1889   Occupation: ?

1881 Census details

The family was living at Highlanders [Upper Tilehouse Street] Father Richard 44, was a miller's yard labourer and he was born in Elton, Hunts. Sarah 43, his wife, (born in Northamptonshire) was a straw plaiter. They had Arthur 19, a machinist (born in Daventry), Richard 17, a bricklayer's labourer (born at Eversdon) and Edward 9, Clara 6 and **Frederick W.** 2 who were all born in Hitchin.

1891 Census details

Richard had now died so widow Sarah 51, now a laundress was living at 3 Queen Street with Edward 19, a hairdresser's assistant and **Frederick W.** 13.

1901 Census details

In 1901 Sarah 61 was living at 10 Garden Row, with only one son, **Frederick W.** 23, who was a blacksmith.

1911 Census details

Frederick Waldron Stimpson, a blacksmith had now been married for 9 years to Ellen 31, who had been born in Southwold. They were living at 84 Hayling's Road, Leiston, Suffolk and had little Frederick W. R. Stimpson their son, who was 4 and had been born in Walkern. They also had a boarder William Jackson 19, a toolmaker living with them.

Military details

Frederick enlisted in 1914 in Leiston (possibly having been in the Territorials). He was entitled to 3 medals but was already in his thirties.

He was number 193 (an early enlistment) in the 4th Battalion Suffolk Regiment which when they went over to France in November 1914 was part of the Jellundur Brigade, Lahore (Indian Division). They were in action at the Battle of Neuve Chapelle earlier in 1915 then again at the Battle of Festubert 15-25th May 1915. The Suffolks were holding the line and giving supporting fire to other attacking battalions on the 16th when sadly Sgt. **Frederick Stimpson** was killed.

Name.		Corps.		Rank.		Regtl. No.
STIMPSON		¼ Suff. R. — " —		Sjt.		193. — " —
	Frederick					

Medal.	Roll.	Page.	Remarks.
VICTORY	K/1/103 B 23	4579	K m A 16. 5. 15
BRITISH	do	do	
14 STAR	K/1/6.	232.	

Theatre of War first served in		
Date of entry therein	8. 11. 14	K. 1380

Evidence by low service number 193, that he enlisted early

He is commemorated on Panel 9 of the Le Touret Memorial to the Missing alongside 13,000 others who fell in the battles in that area before September 1915 and whose bodies were never found/identified. He was 36.

Walter George Stokes

Date of Birth: 29-8-1893
First School: Offley National School
Hitchin Boys' British School
Date of Admission: 28-6-1904
Parents: George (a gardener) and Mary Eliza
Address on admission: Oak Villa, Lancaster Road
Left school: 23-11-1906   Occupation: ?

1901 Census details

The family was living in Offley village, near Hitchin, where father George 48, was a gardener. His wife Mary was 44. She was born in Pineham, Kent but all the family were born in Offley. The children recorded were Arthur 17, Dorothy 15, Marguerite 12, Mark 10, Kathleen 9, **Walter** 7 and Norman 4.

1911 Census details

There were 7 children still at home of the 8 living children. They had lost 2 children and Dorothy was living elsewhere. They had 6 rooms at their new address, 18 Lancaster Road. (possibly Oak Villa).Their middle names were now recorded by their father who had to fill in the census form.

Mary Eliza his wife, was a dressmaker, Herbert Morris 29, had returned home and was a nurseryman, Arthur William 27, was a gardener, Marguerite Emily 22, was at home, Mark Harley 20, was a grocer's assistant, Kathleen Elizabeth 19, was a milliner, **Walter George** 17, was a gardener and Norman Edwin 14, was a tailor's assistant.

From the newspaper cutting of June 16th 1917 we know that Walter was a very "bright and sunny" lad who was intelligent and good-humoured. He was well known in the town being on the staff of the Hitchin Playhouse and also a member of the Hitchin Church Adult class with his brothers. He was said to have sent this institution many messages from the Front, the last one asking everyone to "Look on the bright side of things and keep smiling."

Military details

Walter volunteered for the Royal Field Artillery in October 1915 and went out to France in September 1916. He was Gunner 170890 "D" Battery, 180th Brigade R.F.A.

They provided the artillery support (with 6 inch Howitzer guns) for the 16th (Irish) Infantry Division.

Recently excavated German tunnels on Messines Ridge

122

Before the Battle of Passchendaele (31st July-10th November 1917) could commence, the Allies had to move the enemy from Messines Ridge (just south of Ypres). Before the attack on Messines commenced on June 7th they subjected the ridge to a tremendous artillery bombardment. Between 12 noon on the 1st and noon on the 10th the 2,233 guns of all calibres fired 2,843,163 rounds, (a total weight of 64,164 tons) onto the ridge and its immediate surrounds.

It was on the 5th during this 'softening' procedure that Walter was killed and the gunner alongside him, injured.

Gunner **Walter Stokes** is buried at Kemmel Château Military Cemetery very close to where his gun would have been at the time, in row D, grave 75. He was 23. A visit to his grave on an autumn afternoon in 2013 revealed that the family had arranged for the inscription 'Peace Perfect Peace With Loved Ones Far Away'. He *will* always be remembered.

Headstone inscription

The entrance to Kemmel Château Military Cemetery

Arthur Summerfield (brother of Harold)

Date of Birth: 5-6-1899
First School: Hitchin British Infants' School
Hitchin Boys' British School
Date of Admission: 1-5-1906
Parents: John (a coachman/groom) and Sarah
Address on admission: 18 Old Park Road
Left school: 6-6-1913   Occupation: Errand boy

*Royal Irish Rifles
cap badge*

1901 Census details

The family was living at 18 Old Park Road. John 44, and his
wife Sarah 42 were both born in Westoning, Bedfordshire.
Their children were Fred 19, a coachman/groom, Sidney 17, a gardener, Reginald
14, a houseboy, Cissie 9, Harold 3 and **Arthur** 1.

In 1906, on April 22nd Harold, **Arthur** and Hilda were all baptised at the
Parish Church.

1911 Census details

They were now living at 30 Union Road. [Oughtonhead Way]. John was 54
and Sarah 51. Fred 29, was a chauffeur, Sidney 27, was a fireman on the railway,

The author pays tribute

124

Lilian (Cissie?) 20, was a boot shop assistant, Harold 13, was an errand boy, **Arthur** 11, was a scholar. Young Hilda was 9. They were living in 5 rooms, had been married for 32 years and had 7 of their 8 children still living.

Military details

Arthur enlisted in Bedford and it was thought that he was working for Waters and Sons of Bancroft at the time. He first went into the Royal Warwickshire Regiment (38572) before transferring to the Royal Irish Rifles as Rifleman 52459. His medals entitlement card shows that he went over to Belgium after the beginning of 1916.

In the year in which he died, 1918, his battalion which had been formed from the Antrim Volunteers, had been reinforced with soldiers from other regiments because of their great losses.

May 21st, the opening day of the Spring Offensive was a dreadful day for losses. Young Rifleman **Arthur Summerfield**, who was only 19 was killed on June 6th 1918 a day after his birthday and is buried in the Klein-Vierstraat British Cemetery, plot V, row A, grave 17. This cemetery is south west of Ypres in Belgium and when I paid my respects at his grave, a beautiful red rose shone out in the fading autumn sunshine.

Harold Summerfield (brother of Arthur)
Recorded as Richard in the school register

Date of Birth: 17-7-1897
First School: Hitchin British Infants' School
Hitchin Boys' British School
Date of Admission: 1-5-1903
Parents: Jack, known as John (an ostler) and Sarah
Address on admission: 18 Old Park Road
Left school: 21-7-1911   Occupation: Skin dyer

The census details are the same as for his brother Arthur.

Military details

Harold enlisted in Hitchin and would have been just 17 when war broke out. He and his brother Arthur both joined the colours and perished.

Harold was in the Royal Field Artillery and had 2 numbers, 135777 and 777046. He was in "C" Battery, 282nd (Howitzers) Army Brigade, originally with 56th Division but they were moved to Army control in January 1917.

Harold's service records have not survived but from his medal entitlement it is clear that he did not go over to the front until after the beginning of 1916, after his 18th birthday. A recently uncovered newspaper report of September 1st 1917 says that Dick (as he was known) was employed at Russell's tanyard and enlisted in 1916. He would have undergone training and then joined his battery probably dealing with the horses as he is recorded as a driver and would have been involved with driving the horses that pulled the gun carriages. This was a family tradition it seems, as his father and brother Fred were ostler and groom. Driver **Harold Summerfield** died on August 16th 1917 in the Battle of Langemarck and it seems from a letter to his parents, that it was the result of a bursting shell. A press report on September 8th quoted from the letter to his parents, living at Rising Villas, 30 Union Road. [Oughtonhead Way] from 2nd Lieutenant. J.R. Marshall saying,

'His death was instantaneous so that he knew no pain. His battery was taking part in important operations and was also under shellfire. A shell came within 57 yards of the gun on which your son was working and killed the sergeant and your son, wounding others. I want to express how sorry we are to lose him and how sorry we are for you. Your son's death was a glorious one. How can a man die better than defending his country? I was always fond of your son and he was always willing and hardworking. He was buried in a soldiers' cemetery and we are making a cross for him'.

He was, in fact, due for leave having spent 11 months at the front. He is buried at Duhallow Advanced Dressing Station Cemetery, plot 1, row B, grave 13 and was one of the first burials there as the cemetery was only started in July 1917. He was aged 20 years 1 month. He is buried alongside 22 year old Sergeant F.Corby referred to in the letter to his parents.

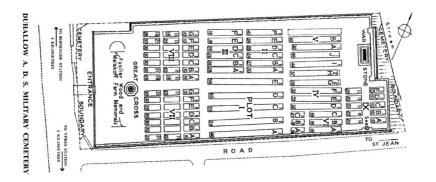

Plot 1, Row B Grave 13 marks his final resting place

George Walter Tansley

Date of Birth: 8-10-1885
First School: Hitchin British Infants' School
Hitchin Boys' British School
Date of Admission: 10-7-1893
Parents: George W. (a gardener) and Emma
Address on admission: Bethel Lane [St John's Road]
Left school: ?   Occupation: ?

1891 Census details

The family was living at 11 Corries Yard. George W. the father was 29 and a gardener, (born in Hitchin in 1862 and the son of William Tansley), Emma his wife was 32, (born in St Ippolyts) and they had 2 children, **George W.** 5, (born in St Ippolyts) and Lily 1, (born in Hitchin).

1901 Census details

They were now living at 6, Park Street and George was a 'carman'. Emma was 42. Young **George** 15, was an errand boy and they had Alfred Bowler as a boarder who was a labourer on the railways.

1911 Census details

George (senior) was now 49 and a 'Hawker in oil', Emma 52, was recorded as doing housework, **George** 25, was a confectioner and Lily 21, was a book folder. The parents had been married for 26 years and had had 2 children. They were still living in 6 rooms at 6 Park Street.

In 1912 young **George** married Annie Margaret Ginger in the final quarter of the year.

Military details

George enlisted in the 3rd Battalion Buffs (East Kent Regiment) as Pte. 21063. This, it seems was a reserve battalion which was stationed in Dover throughout the war and did not go abroad. So I conclude that 31 year old **George** died there on March 15th 1917. On a family grave in Hitchin Cemetery, S.E. Extension 741, it certainly states that he died in Dover. As he did not go abroad he would not have received campaign medals. He was 31.

The Tansley family grave in Hitchin Cemetery

127

Francis Ralph Tarrier

Date of Birth: 7-9-1897
First School: Hitchin British Infants' School
Hitchin Boys' British School
Date of Admission: 2-5-1904
Parents: William and Emma
Address on admission: 31 Grove Road
Left school: 3-8-1911   Occupation: Errand boy

1901 Census details

The family was living at Providence Terrace, Highbury, where William, 38 born in Holwell (Beds) was recorded as a carpenter. His wife Emma 36, (born in Pirton) had 5 children to care for. Frederick, 15, was a gardener, (born in Pirton) Ida 14 and Walter 12 were born in Ickleford, Archie 8 and **Francis Ralph** 3, were born in Pirton.

1911 Census details

The family was living at 4 Diamond Jubilee Terrace, in 4 rooms.

Father William 48, was a carpenter. Emma his wife was 47 and they had been married for 26 years. Their children, still living at home were Frederick 25, a gardener, Walter 22, a carpenter for a builder, Archie 18, a 'coach smith apprentice', **Francis** 13, a schoolboy and Winnie 7.

When **Francis** left school he became an apprentice to Mr J. Cain, the Coach Builder in Queen Street, no doubt following his brother Archie.

Military details

He enlisted on November 15th 1915 at Ampthill and joined the Bedfordshire Regiment as a Pte. 23269 in the 2nd Battalion. After training he went to France in January 1917.

In early April 1917, the battalion was employed in digging communication trenches and Francis wrote his last letter on 6th when he was in billets at Blairville.

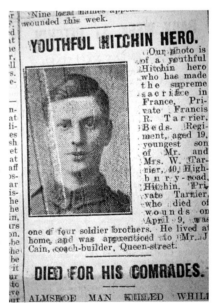

Nine local names appear
wounded this week.

YOUTHFUL HITCHIN HERO.

Our photo is of a youthful Hitchin hero who has made the supreme sacrifice in France. Private R. Tarrier, Beds. Regiment, aged 19, youngest son of Mr. and Mrs. W. Tarrier, 40, High-bury-road, Hitchin. Private Tarrier, who died of wounds on April 9, was one of four soldier brothers. He lived at home, and was apprenticed to Mr. J Cain, coach-builder, Queen-street.

DIED FOR HIS COMRADES.

ALMSHOE MAN KILLED WHILE

The war diary extract for the date that he died follows;

9 Apr 1917 [The Battle of Arras - the First Battle of the Scarpe] - St-Martin-sur-Cojeul At 1.30 am "D" Company under 2nd Lieut.J.P. Pitts[James P. PITTS, MC] attacked StMARTIN-SUR-COJEUL. At the same time "C" Coy under Capt.R.E.Oakley [Robert Edwin OAKLEY, MC] pushed forward on flanks and established posts at N.33.d.3/9 and N.27.c.1/5. After "D" Coy had cleared ST MARTIN 2nd Lieut.A.F. Aldridge [Arthur Frederick ALDRIDGE] of "C" Coy established a post holding one Platoon at N.33.a.7/6. Casualties Lieut. W.E.HART, slightly wounded, 2 O.R. wounded. We captured prisoners of 86th R.I.R.. "D" Company withdrew to SWITCH LANE about 5 am remainder of morning quiet and spent in fitting and resting At 5.30 am General Attack on the LEFT commenced. At 2 pm attack by our Brigade started. 19th BN. K.L.R. Attacking on the RIGHT. 20th Bn.K.L.R. Attacking on the LEFT. 2nd Bn.Bedfordshire R. In Support. 17th Bn.K.L.R. In Reserve. "A" and "D" Companies were supporting 19th Bn.K.L.R. SOUTH of River COJEUL. "B" Company supporting 19th and 20th Bn.K.L.R. NORTH of River COJEUL. "C" Company in Posts at St MARTIN and In Reserve. Enemy put up fairly strong barrage in HENIN. "B" Company avoided Casualties by keeping to left of Village.

Francis was injured on April 9th and died and was buried the same day according to information received from Mr T.E. Brookes of the Herts Local Committee, who no doubt sought extra information from regiments for families waiting at home.

Pte. **Francis Tarrier** who was only 19, was buried at the Crucifix at Henin-sur-Cojeul according to these records but his name is on the Arras Memorial to the Missing, Bay 5, so his last resting place was no doubt lost in all the shelling that ensued on that terrain. The family must have been devastated knowing that 3 other sons were also fighting for their country, according to the newspaper report of June 2nd 1917.

Carved in stone

George Tomlin

South Wales Borderers cap badge

Date of Birth: 14-2-1882
First School: Sunnyside School
Hitchin Boys' British School
Date of Admission: 23-9-1889
Parents: ? Uncle Harry seemed to be the guardian
Address on admission: Hitchin Hill
Left school: 15-7-1895   Occupation: ?

1891 census details

The family lived at 46 Hitchin Hill where Harry 23, was a bricklayer. His wife Eliza Ann was 25. Young Dorothy Lilian 3, George Harry 1 and nephew **George** aged 9 (born in Newcastle) were at home.

1901 Census details

Harry was now 32 and his wife Eliza was recorded as 31 and born in Leicester. Young George H. was 11, Alice was 9 and Lucy M. had arrived. There was also recorded a nephew Harry 17 also born in Newcastle but **George** had left home.

1911 Census details

George can now be tracked to Woolmer Green, Knebworth as the Harry in the 1901 census is now 26 and married to Florence 24, (born in Hinxworth). His brother **George** now 28 was lodging with them and was recorded as a regular soldier in the South Wales Borderers which matches the military research. They also had a little nephew, Harry 5, (also born in Newcastle) living with them

Military details

As a regular soldier 8694 in the 1st Battalion South Wales Borderers he was in Borden, Hants. when war was declared. He was no doubt in training but left Southampton with his regiment on August 12th 1914 on board S.S. "Gloucester Castle"

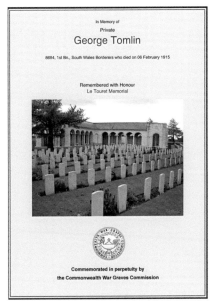

In Memory of
Private
George Tomlin
8694, 1st Bn., South Wales Borderers who died on 06 February 1915

Remembered with Honour
Le Touret Memorial

Commemorated in perpetuity by
the Commonwealth War Graves Commission

C.W.G.C. Certificate

arriving in Le Havre on 13th. According to the medal rolls index he was awarded the 3 Great War medals. The qualifying date for the 1914 Star was August 5th-November 22nd No service records have survived.

There was no Divisional History written post- war for the first Division of which his regiment was a part right through the war so little can be gleaned of his 7 months in action but we do know that his battalion went out of line on February 3rd 1915 and returned on 24th. Pte.**George Tomlin** was killed on the 6th of that month so perhaps he was killed by a long-range shell. The 1st Division was certainly involved in all the bloody battles of the early months of the war and **George** would have had a dreadful time. He was 32.

His name appears on the Le Touret Memorial to the Missing, Panels 14-15.

Oswald Leslie Tomlin

Date of Birth: 30-1-1898
First School: Hitchin British Infants' School
Hitchin Boys' British School
Date of Admission: 12-5-1904
Parents: James (a bricklayer) and Mary Ann
Address on admission: 3 Hitchin Hill
Left school: 21-12-1911
Occupation: Telegraph messenger

Royal Engineers cap badge

1901 Census details

Father James 47, a bricklayer and his wife Mary Ann 48, (born St Ippolyts) were living at 3 Hitchin Hill with their children Florence 22, Norman Percy 17, a bricklayer, Frank 15, an errand boy (post), Stanley 13, Mabel 11, Harold 9, Wilfred 6 and **Oswald Leslie** 3. All were born in Hitchin.

1911 Census details

The family remained at the same address with father James still working. Wilfred was now a butcher, **Leslie** was an errand boy and Claude 8, had been born. They had had 11 children and 10 were still living. They had 5 rooms available to them.

Military details

Oswald Leslie enlisted in Hitchin as 75366 Sapper A.N. Cable Section, Royal Engineers. According to the Medal Rolls Index he qualified for the 15 Star

A moving family tribute

plus the War and Victory medals so his entry date onto the battlefields of December 1915 made him just short of his 18th birthday.

Sapper Tomlin was sadly killed on July 1st 1916, aged 18, somewhere in the Ypres area of Belgium, as he is buried in Brandhoek Military Cemetery, plot II, row F, grave 14.

He was part of the Signal Section so he could have been anywhere in the area. On visiting his grave one evening I found a touching inscription, 'In Heaven To Meet Again, Father, Mother, Brothers and Sisters Love' which would have cost them over 13 shillings at 3 ½ pence per letter, a lot of money in those days. One hopes that a member of the family was able to visit his grave.

Bertie Watson

Date of Birth: 13-10-1893
First School: Hitchin British Infants' School
Hitchin Boys' British School
Date of Admission: 21-5-1900
Parents: Charles (a coal carter) and Emma
Address on admission: Charlton

Left school: 11-10-1907

Occupation: Errand boy

1901 Census details

Father Charles 42 (born in St Ippolyts) was a coal carter. His wife Emma was 40 and they had Frank 12, **Bertie** 7 and Arthur 1. The family was living in Charlton on the outskirts of Hitchin.

1911 Census details

Charles was 52, and Emma was 50. **Bertie** now 17, was a farm labourer, Arthur was 11 and Elsie 8, had arrived. They were still in Charlton.

Military details

Bertie enlisted in Hitchin in the 6th Battalion Bedfordshire Regiment. After training he went to France on 30th September 1915 as the medal rolls index indicates so he was awarded the 1914-15 Star and the War and Victory medals.

October and November were extremely wet months according to the Regimental War Diaries so conditions got worse and worse as they dug and repaired trenches in working parties and put up wire entanglements in the area between Souastre and Hannescamps.

According to the details, trench foot was a dreadful problem and grease was issued for the troops to rub into their painful feet. The water in the trenches was knee deep!

The lead up to Christmas was equally cold and miserable and only helped at times when the boys were relieved for some rest and recuperation behind the lines. Continuous artillery activity added to the misery and 1916 started in a similar fashion with little movement until June/July in the lead up to the Battle of the Somme (July 1st) They then seemed to be in the thick of the battle with daily casualties being recorded until the August 17th when 288 fresh soldiers and 5 officers arrived so **Bertie's** battalion was moved back up north to Mazingarbe, near Loos.

On August 26th the war diary states that '2 other ranks were killed and 6 wounded' and we know that Pte. Bertie Watson was wounded and he died later that day aged 22.

He is buried at Philosophie Cemetery in Mazingarbe plot I, row J, grave 6.

Cecil Weare

Date of Birth: 22-5-1893
First School: Hitchin British Infants' School
Hitchin Boys' British School
Date of Admission: 21-5-1900
Parents: Frederick (a watchmaker) and Alice
Address on admission: 14 Tilehouse Street
Left school: 7-6-1907
Occupation: Engineer

Canadian cap badge

1901 Census details

Frederick, his father (born Wincanton, Somerset), age 42, a watchmaker and Alice (née Parker) 36, were living at 14 Tilehouse Street with Evelyn 14, Raymond 13, Elsie 12, **Cecil** 7, Infant Weare, 3 weeks and Alice's mother Maria 60, a dressmaker.

1911 Census details

Cecil 17, was now a 'hall boy' in the employ of Frances A. Delmé Radcliffe 65, Commander Royal Navy (Ret.) J.P. at The Priory, Hitchin which was said to have had 50 rooms and needed a large number of staff..

Military details

The newspaper report of November 10th1917 gives a fairly full account of his service.
He went to Canada in about 1913 and his attestation papers show that he joined up as a Private on 5th December 1914 in Halifax, Nova Scotia in the 25th Battalion Canadian Infantry (Nova Scotia Regiment). He had been living with an aunt, Gertrude Lanning in Ladner, British Columbia.

He went over to France in September 1915 where he quickly gained promotion and was made a Lieutenant in October 1915. According to a newspaper report (October 12th 1916) his mother had had a letter from him saying:

"We have been through an awful charge and we have made our name, although we were badly cut up. Sir Douglas Haig said that it was 'A piece of work unparalleled in the history of war.' On that day I earned my commission.

Canadian Medical Record for Cecil Weare M.C.

He suffered from shell shock and lost the hearing in his left ear in the taking of Vimy Ridge on April 9th 1917 in that dreadful battle when so many Canadians lost their lives.

For his bravery in this action he was awarded the Military Cross and promoted to Captain at age 23 and 11 months! This was announced in the London Gazette on July 18th 1917.

Lt. Cecil Weare, Canadian Infy.
For conspicuous gallantry and devotion to duty. "He led his company in the face of heavy fire of all kinds, and, despite strong opposition, captured and consolidated the enemy trench. He displayed great courage and initiative throughout."

Because of his condition he was made 'conducting officer' at the base and given lighter duties. In October he took troops up the line to Ypres and there he met up with his brother Lance Corporal Raymond Weare, who had also been a pupil of our school. They had not met since April of the previous year when they were at Ypres together.

He left his brother that evening in order to sleep in billets that night with his fellow officers and in the early hours of the next day, October 31st, the hut was hit by an aerial bomb that severely wounded him. At 6 am he was received into the casualty clearing station where sadly he died at 9.25 that morning being conscious to the last. The Sister-in-charge wrote to his mother and said that her son had suffered very little pain at the end.

What a sad loss of this brilliant young officer to his family and his regiment. He was 24.

CAPTAIN CECIL WEARE, M.C

KILLED BY AERIAL BOMB.

It is with deep regret we report the death in action, on October 31, of Captain Cecil Weare, M.C., second son of Mr. and Mrs. F. W. Weare, 5, Park-street, Hitchin. This gallant young officer joined the Canadian Forces in October, 1914, as a private. He was sent to France in September, 1915, where he quickly gained promotion, and in October, 1916, was made lieutenant. He received shell shock at the taking of Vimy Ridge, on April 9, 1917. For his bravery in this action he was promoted to Captain, and was awarded the Military Cross. On this occasion he lost the hearing of his left ear, and so was made conducting officer at the base. When he met his death he had taken troops up the line to Ypres, where he met his brother, Lance-Corpl. Raymond Weare, who had that day returned from leave in Hitchin. They had not met since April, 1916, when they were at Ypres together. Leaving his brother during the evening, Captain Weare went to spend the night in a hut, in which some officers were quartered, prior to his returning to the base the following day. In the early hours of the morning the hut was struck by an aerial bomb, severely wounding him. He was received into the clearing station at 6 a.m., and passed away at 9.25 the same morning, being conscious to the last. A letter received by his mother from the Sister-in-charge, stated that he suffered very little pain. He had recently returned from leave. The loss of this brilliant officer has evoked great sympathy in the town, where the family are highly esteemed, and the family have received the condolences of many friends.

Herts. Express November 10 1917

135

Captain **Cecil Weare M.C.** is buried in Lijssenthoek Military Cemetery just west of Ypres in Belgium, plot XXI, row AA, grave 14. The Canadian maple leaf stood out on his grave in this vast cemetery where most of the burials were of men who would have died of wounds in the casualty clearing station near by.

Frederick John Whaley

Date of Birth: 11-8-1882
First School: Private School
Hitchin Boys' British School
Date of Admission: 15-7-1889
Parents: William and Eliza
Address on admission: Bedford Road
Left school: 19-6-1897   Occupation: ?

1891 Census details

The family lived at 14 Bedford Road. and Father William 40, (born in St Ives, Hunts.) was a hairdresser. His wife Eliza was 38, (born in Holwell, Herts.) and they had 5 children. William Foster was 10, **Frederick John** was 8, Florence Mabel was 6, Lilly Victoria was 4 and Eva Eliza was 2. They had a 21 year old domestic servant, Sarah A. Collins helping them in the house too.

1901 Census details

Father William was still a hairdresser and William was his assistant. Mother Eliza now 38 had had Gladys Mary 9, and Percy Hugh 4, since the last census, with all the children except our **Frederick** still living at home.

Frederick, now 19 was a boarder at 1 Broadway, South Wimbledon and was an outfitter's assistant.

1911 Census details

In this census record, made on April 2nd **Frederick** was boarding at Portland House, 18 Portland Road. Southsea (Hants.) and was a hosier salesman (possibly with Messrs Handley). He was living in a very large boarding house.

Military details

He enlisted in 1915 in Portsmouth in the Royal Field Artillery (2096) and as his medal entitlement indicates two medals it would seem that he went over to France after the beginning of 1916.

A tranquil setting at Ecoivres Military Cemetery

He was on an 18 pounder field gun. His artillery brigade was giving artillery cover for the 60th (2nd/2nd) London Infantry Regiment. July and August 1916 saw the Division on the western side of the approaches to Vimy Ridge near Arras and **Frederick** and his colleagues kept up a series of concentrated artillery bombardments on specified sections of the enemy front line. Obviously the enemy retaliated in kind and they were exceptionally well equipped with heavy mortars and artillery of various sizes and were well dug in.

Driver **Frederick John Whaley's** gun team was probably situated not far from where he lies buried at Ecoivres Military Cemetery in plot 111, row C, grave 23. His death occurred on August 6th 1916 when he was 33 years of age. Buried alongside him is another soldier killed on the same day in his unit. I visited his grave on a beautiful summer's evening and found the inscription 'Rest In The Lord' on his headstone.

'Rest in the Lord'

Walter Charles Wilson

Date of Birth: 15-7-1897
First School: Hitchin British Infants' School
Hitchin Boys' British School
Date of Admission: 2-5-1904
Parents: Charles and Emma
Address on admission: Oughton Head Cottages
Left school: 14-7-1911   Occupation: Errand boy

1901 Census details

Father Charles, 35 and Emma 42, were living at Oughton Head Cottages
with Lizzie 7 and **Walter Charles** 3. They had 2 boarders, William and Joseph
Twydell, 17 and 48 respectively.

1911 Census details

Charles was now recorded as 40? and was a farm labourer and Emma was 53.
They had been married for 18 years. Lizzie aged 17, was a domestic servant,
Walter 13, was still at school and Joseph was still a boarder. They were now
living at 2 Taylor's Cottages, Old Park Road.

Military details

Walter enlisted in Hitchin applying to
join the Territorial Army on January
6th 1914 as Pte. 2314 and at his medical
on 27th January he was said to be 17
yrs. 6 months, 5 feet 4 inches tall with a
fully expanded girth of 32 ½ inches. He
was working as an agricultural labourer
for a Mr Hailey in Gt. Wymondley. He
was 'embodied' on August 5th 1914
in the 1st Herts Regiment (265387)
and after training went to France on
August 21st 1916 He was wounded
on October 5th 1916 and went back
to England to recover. He returned to
France March 21st 1917 His battalion
was part of the 116th Brigade, 39th
Division at the time of his death aged
20 on April 25th 1918. This was at
the 2nd Battle of Kemmel Ridge, near
Ypres, Belgium in the last big German

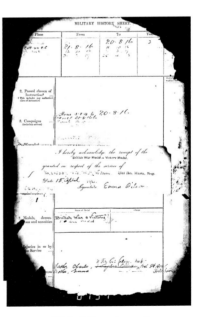

Walter's 'burnt' records

push in that area in that year. Private **Walter Wilson's** body was undiscovered so his name is to be found on the vast Tyne Cot Memorial to the Missing, Panel 153. His medals were the T.F. and the War and Victory medals.

Panel 153 at Tyne Cot

Arthur Worbey

Date of Birth: 3-12-1893
First School: St Saviour's
Hitchin Boys' British School
Date of Admission: 1-5-1902
Parents: Arthur (a GNR platelayer) and Martha
Address on admission: 15 Anderson's Row
Left school: 19-12-1907
Occupation: Bookstall boy

*Duke of Cornwall's
Light Infantry cap badge*

1901 Census details

The family was living at 15 Anderson's Row, Florence Street. Father Arthur 29, was a railway platelayer and his wife Martha (Mary?) was 31. They had **Arthur William** 7, Gertrude 6, Charles 4 and Ethel 11 months. All the children were born when they were living in Cambridgeshire.

1911 Census details

15 Anderson's Row was still the address of the family. Young **Arthur William** who was now 17 was a bricklayer's labourer, Gertrude was a bookbinder, Charles was a 'time lad', Ethel was 10, Doris Edith was 8 and Lilian was 6.

Military details

Arthur William Worbey signed up for the Territorial Army when aged 18 years and one month on January 12th, 1912. His pension records have survived so we know that he was a diminutive 5 feet 2 ¼ inches and had a chest measurement of 33 ½ inches. He enlisted in the 1st Battalion Herts Regiment with the No.1780. Arthur was in training but was set down on August 8th, 1914, (4 days after the outbreak of the Great War). He was said to be "medically ufit for further military service" after 2 years and 209 days.

He obviously re-enlisted when reinforcements were desperately needed and was accepted into the Herts.Regiment again. His service number was 3774. According to his medals entitlement card he transferred into the 6th Battalion Duke of Cornwall's Light Infantry at some point with the No. 28715 but because we don't know when that was, it is impossible to know his military actions, only that he went over to France after the beginning of 1916 when he was 22. He was part of the 43rd Brigade in the 14th Division.

In September 1916 they were in action on the Somme. On the 16th, 4 companies of the 6th Duke of Cornwall's Light Infantry were to support 10th Durham Light Infantry in action between Flers and Gueudecourt but the day did not go well. The advance group came under heavy fire when our artillery bombardment appeared to be very weak and did not creep forward ahead of the troops.

The 6th Duke of Cornwall's Light Infantry were the reinforcements and they lost heavily in the push forwards. At the end of the day the 43rd Brigade's battalion commanders were highly critical of the inadequate artillery support. Thus casualties in the brigade that day were 67 officers and 1,366 men.

In the days that followed, operations were mainly focussed on reorganisation and consolidation ready for the next advance and eventually the 14th Division was relieved but not before our Pte. **Arthur Worbey** was killed in action. His death occurred on September 19th 1916 and, because of

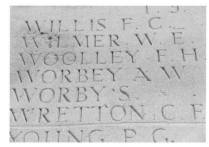

Remembered with Pride

all the action over that ground, his body was not found/identified and therefore he is commemorated on the Thiepval Memorial to the Missing, Pier and Face 6B. He was 22.

Christopher Wright

Date of Birth: 28-8-1900
First School: St Saviour's
Hitchin Boys' British School
Date of Admission: 1-5-1908
Parents: Edmund (a gas fitter) and Selina
Address on admission: 93 Walsworth Road
Left school: ?   Occupation: ?

1901 Census details

The family was living at 9 Benslow Lane and father Edmund aged 48, was a gas fitter. Selina his wife was 39 and they had Edmund C. 19, Harold 13, Fred 11 and **Christopher** 7 months. They were all Hitchin born.

1911 Census details

They were now living at 84 Walsworth Road. Edmund was still a gas fitter and Selina had more children to look after, as new names appear which indicate they were away from home in 1901. Mildred was 26, Harold 23, was now a machine minder, Fred 21, was a commercial traveller, Douglas 16, was a clerk and young **Chris** was still at school. They had 2 boarders, Robert Vallance and Reg Gardiner.

Military details

This young man enlisted as Rifleman TR/13/84514, 10th Battalion Rifle Brigade but was in training with the 53rd Y.S. Battalion Rifle Brigade (Young Soldiers) when he died aged 18, in hospital in Northampton of influenza, which turned to pneumonia.

*Rifleman Christopher Wright,
Herts Express October 20 1918*

Full details of his military funeral were reported in the *Herts Express* newspaper on October 20th 1918. Rifleman **Chris Wright** is buried in the Hitchin Cemetery S. 960.

May They All Rest In Peace

TIMELINE 1914-1919

1914	June 28th	Archduke Franz Ferdinand of Austria assassinated in Sarajevo
	July 5th	Kaiser Wilhelm II promised German support for Austria against Serbia
	July 28th	Austria declared war on Serbia
	August 1st	Germany declared war on Russia
	August 3/4th	Germany declared war on France and invaded Belgium
		Britain declared war on Germany and landed first troops in France on 7th
	August 23rd	The BEF started to retreat from Mons and ended Sept. 5th
		Germany invaded France
	September 6th	Start of the Battle of the Marne
	October 18th	First Battle of Ypres to November 22nd
	November 2nd	Russia declared war on Turkey as Turkey had entered the war on Germany's side on October 28th
		Trench warfare started to dominate the Western Front
	December 24th	The Christmas Truce, a short respite in some areas before fighting re-commenced. Princess Mary's gifts to the troops were distributed
1915	January 19th	The first Zeppelin raid on Britain took place
	February 19th	Britain bombarded the Turkish forts in the Dardanelles. Attacks repulsed March 18th
	April 22nd	The 2nd Battle of Ypres until May 14th
	April 25th	Allied troops landed in Gallipoli (Turkey)
	May 7th	The "Lusitania" was sunk by a German U-boat
	May 23rd	Italy declared war on Germany and Austria
	August 5th	The Germans captured Warsaw from the Russians

	September 25th	The start of the Battle of Loos (France) until October 5th
	December 7th	The Siege of Kut began (Mesopotamia)
	December 19th	The Allies started the evacuation of Gallipoli
1916	January 27th	Conscription began in Great Britain
	February 21st	Start of the Battle of Verdun
	April 29th	British forces surrendered to Turks at Kut
	May 31st	Battle of Jutland
	June 5th	Lord Kitchener, the British Secretary of State for War, drowned. Succeeded by Mr Lloyd George on July 7th
	July 1st	The start of the Battle of the Somme. Brodie tin helmets were made general issue with a million being distributed this summer
	September 15th	The first use of tanks en masse at the Somme
	December 7th	Mr Lloyd George became British Prime Minister succeeding Mr Asquith
1917	February 1st	Germany's unrestricted submarine campaign started
	March 12th	Russian Revolution began with the Tsar abdicating on 15th
	April 6th	USA declared war on Germany
	April 9th	Battles of Arras began (Vimy Ridge 9th - 14th)
	April 16th	France launched an unsuccessful offensive on the Western Front
	June 7th	Battle of Messines
	July 31st	Battles of Ypres began (Passchendaele) – November 10th
	November 6th	Britain launched a major offensive on the Western Front
	November 20th	Battle of Cambrai. British tanks won a victory
	November 21st	Bolshevik government in Russia and 'Central Powers' began armistice talks (Germany, the Austrian Hungarian Empire, the Ottoman Empire and Bulgaria)

	December 9th	Britain captured Jerusalem from the Turks
1918	March 21st	Germany broke through on the Somme
	March 29th	Marshal Foch appointed Allied Commander on the Western Front
	April 9th	Germany began an offensive in Flanders
	July 15th	The second Battle of the Marne started which triggered the start of the collapse of the German army
	August 8th	The 'Last 100 Days' starts when the advancing Allies succeed
	September 19th	Turkish forces collapsed at Megiddo (Palestine)
	October 4th	Germany asked the Allies for an armistice
	October 29th	Germany's navy mutinied
	October 30th	Armistice between Turkey and the Entente Powers signed (Great Britain, France and Russia)
	November 3rd	Austria made peace
	November 9th	Kaiser Wilhelm II abdicated
	November 11th	Deserted by her allies and being driven back to her own frontier, Germany signed an armistice with the Allies and hostilities ceased. The official end of the Great War
1919	January 4th	The Peace Conference met in Paris
	June 21st	The surrendered German naval fleet at Scapa Flow was scuttled
	June 28th	The Treaty of Versailles was signed by the Germans. They very reluctantly had to agree to make substantial territorial concessions and pay reparations totalling 132 billion Marks, equivalent to £284 billion pounds today

Focus on the Facts

We lost 68 'Old Boys':

8 were married
36 were killed in action (KIA)
15 died of wounds abroad (DOW)
4 drowned
11 died of wounds or Spanish Flu in Britain
2 died of Spanish Flu in prisoner of war camps

December 1914 recruiting poster

Spanish Flu

The 1918 flu pandemic was unusually deadly and affected almost 50 million people throughout the world, killing between 3% and 5%. It struck many young fit adults which again was unusual so during the latter years of the Great War many troops were smitten. There was health censorship in the war torn countries but not in neutral Spain so, the nickname became the Spanish Flu or the Grippe. Étaples in France, being a big troop training area and hospital complex was thought by one leading British virologist to be the centre of the 1918 outbreak but this is uncertain.

Dealing with the wounded

In simple terms the route for an injured soldier, depending on his condition would be, Aid Post — Field Ambulance — Main or Advanced Dressing Station — Casualty Clearing Station — Base Hospital- General Hospital e.g. Rouen, Étaples- Hospital or Convalescent Home in the UK. When ambulant in UK the injured soldiers were given distinctive blue uniforms with red ties to denote they were injured and not malingering. One of the biggest problems with returning military was 'shell shock' due to their dreadful experiences. (See http://www.1914-1918.net/wounded.htm)

Where they lie

31 are buried abroad in Commonwealth War Graves Cemeteries

Commonwealth War Graves Commission

Fabian Ware became the commander of a mobile unit of the British Red Cross in France during the war. Saddened by the sheer number of casualties, he felt driven to find a way to ensure the final resting places of the dead would not be lost forever. Under his dynamic leadership, his unit began recording and caring for all the graves they could find. By 1915, their work was given official recognition by the War Office and incorporated into the British Army as the Graves Registration Commission.

In May 1917, the Imperial War Graves Commission was established by Royal Charter and Fabian Ware was made Vice-Chairman. The Commission's work began in earnest after the Armistice. Once land for cemeteries and memorials had been guaranteed, the enormous task of recording the details of the dead began. By 1918, some 587,000 graves had been identified and a further 559,000 casualties were registered as having no known grave. Key people involved in the design of memorials, cemeteries and planting schemes were Sir Edwin Lutyens, Sir Reginald Blomfield and garden designer Gertrude Jekyll.

Headstones are simple and standard and made of Portland stone generally, though in some countries local stone is used. In areas susceptible to earthquakes or strong winds, they are smaller and laid flat. The gardeners of the Commission do an excellent job and in all but one of the hundred or more cemeteries that I have visited their loving care really showed. The Commission is currently responsible for the care of war dead at over 23,000 separate burial sites in 153 different countries and the maintenance of more than 200 memorials worldwide. In addition to commemorating Commonwealth military service members, the Commission maintains, under arrangement with applicable governments, over 40,000 non-Commonwealth war graves and over 25,000 non-war military and civilian graves.

Eleven are buried in Hitchin Cemetery, most with Commonwealth War Graves Commission headstones.

26 are named on the following Memorials

The Menin Gate Memorial to the Missing, Ypres, Belgium 7
Thiepval Memorial to the Missing, Somme, France 3
Tyne Cot Memorial to the Missing, Ypres, Belgium 3

Recruiting poster

Arras Memorial to the Missing, France 3
Le Touret Memorial to the Missing, France 2
Cambrai Memorial to the Missing, Louveral, France1
Loos Memorial to the Missing, France 1
Pozières Memorial to the Missing, France 1
Vimy Ridge Memorial to the Missing, France 1
Chatby Memorial to the Missing, Egypt 1
Plymouth Naval Memorial to the Missing, Devon 1
Chatham Naval Memorial to the Missing, Kent, England 2
Also their names are recorded on the Hitchin War Memorial and in other locations that I have visited in the town.

64 lads joined the army
4 lads joined the navy
2 died in 1914
7 died in 1915
16 died in 1916
22 died in 1917
20 died in 1918
1 died in 1919

The very youngest was Pte. Harold Barker with two more 18 year olds, Stoker Herbert Edward Brandon and Pte. George Ryall.

The oldest was Pte. William Maynard Dimmock who was 41.

5 families lost 2 sons

The Fosters
The Grants
The Greens
The Hunts
The Summerfields

Four of our schoolmasters went off to war, Harold Bates Brant, Ernest Edward Dennis, Leonard Stokes Hart and Solomon T. Hill. Two thirds of their salary was paid to them on war service and they all returned to teach at the school.

Our boys were in the following regiments:

The Australian Tunnelling Company 1
The Bedfordshire Regiment 16
The Canadian Infantry 2
The Dragoon Guards (Prince of Wales' Own) 1
The Duke of Cambridge's Own (Middlesex Regiment) 2
The Duke of Cornwall's Light Infantry 1
The Duke of Wellington's West Riding Regiment 1

The East Kent Regiment 2
The East Surrey Regiment 2
The Essex Regiment 2
The Gloucestershire Regiment 1
The Hertfordshire Regiment 7
The Machine Gun Corps 1
The Middlesex Regiment 2
The Queen's Royal West Surrey Regiment 3
The Rifle Brigade 2
The Royal Berkshire Regiment 1
The Royal Engineers 2
The Royal Field Artillery 3
The Royal Fusiliers 4
The Royal Garrison Artillery 2
The Royal Irish Rifles 1
The South Wales Borderers 1
The Suffolk Regiment 2
The Tank Corps 1
The Welsh Guards 1
The Royal Navy 4

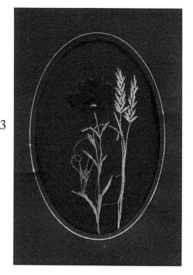

Embroidered for author
by Jenny Rutterford

The origins of the poppy emblem

Lt. Col. John McRae a Canadian medical officer, was so moved by the death and burial of his friend in early 1915 that he was inspired to write his famous poem 'In Flanders Field'. As he stood there at his graveside at St. Mary's Dressing Station Cemetery near the Ypres-Yser canal in Belgium, he looked out across the devastated landscape and noticed red poppies were blooming in the disturbed soil around the graves.

In 1918 an American lady, Prof. Moina Michael was so moved by the poem and its symbolism that she made it her mission to have the poppy adopted as the memorial flower. Thanks to the support of Earl Haig who saw early poppies being sold in a London street she certainly achieved her ambition!

He subsequently became the co-founder of the Royal British Legion. Today, the R.B.L. produces over 40 million poppies a year, raising funds to support veterans and active members of the armed forces.

British Army Structure

British forces were made up from the United Kingdom, the self governing Dominions, India and the Colonial Empire.

An army was made up of a number of Corps.

A Corps was made up of a number of divisions.
An infantry division was made up of a number of brigades (usually 3 or 4).
An infantry brigade was made up of a number of battalions (usually 4).
An infantry battalion was made up of 4 companie.s
An infantry company was made up of 4 platoons.

An infantry regiment had a number of battalions but these did not often serve together, but were split among brigades. An infantry regiment may contain any number of battalions, but usually around 12 - 15. Each would take its place in a brigade as outlined above.

Royal Engineers (R.E.), Royal Artillery (R.A.) and Machine Gun
Companies (M.G.C.) etc.were attached to
divisions.

Army 40,000 men commanded by (General)
Corps 20,000 men (Lieutenant General)
Division 10-12,000 men (Major General)
Brigade 3-4000 men (Brigadier General)
Battalion 800-1000 men (Lieutenant
Colonel)
Companies 160-200 men (Captain)
Platoons 40-50 men (Lieutenant)
Sections 10-14 men (Lance Corporal)
(Approximate numbers)

Army Ranks

Private, Lance Corporal, Corporal, Sergeant, Company Sergeant Major, Regimental Sergeant Major

Commissioned officers
Second Lieutenant, Lieutenant, Captain, Major, Lieutenant Colonel, Colonel, Brigadier General,

From an illustrated Christmas card by W. Smeed in the author's collection

Major General, Lieutenant General, General, Field Marshal

The Territorial Force

Up to 1908, Britain had a tradition of organising local part-time military units known as the Militia and the Volunteers. These had often been created during times of national crisis but with the exception of service during the Boer War in South Africa (1899-1902) had generally remained at home as part-time, local defence, units. The 1908 army reforms carried out by Minister of War Richard Burdon Haldane, hotly debated and not universally agreed, essentially did away with these old units and replaced them with the Territorial Force. It remained a part-time form of soldiering whose stated role was home defence. Men were not obliged to serve overseas, although they could agree to do so. The T.F. was mobilised for full-time service immediately war was declared and members were asked to sign to agree to overseas service.

Voluntary enlistment from 1914 did not provide sufficient numbers for the fighting force so conscription was instituted in January 1916, providing for the call up of single men aged 18–41; in May conscription was extended to married men. Calculating for the whole of the war, conscripts made up a majority of British serving soldiers.

Our Allies

Britain & its Empire, (including Australia, New Zealand, Canada, India, South Africa, W. Indies), France, Russia, Serbia and eventually Italy and the USA fought together, providing the main effort.

Japan participated in World War I from 1914 to 1918 in an alliance with the Entente Powers in support of the Allies and played an important role in securing the sea-lanes in the South Pacific and Indian Ocean against the German navy.

China also declared war on Germany in 1917 and thousands from that land worked as an invaluable labour corps backing up our fighting troops.

'The Iron Harvest'

Great War Medals

When the WW1 medals were issued in the 1920's it coincided with a popular comic strip published by the Daily Mirror newspaper. It was written by Bertram J. Lamb ('Uncle Dick'), and drawn by the cartoonist Austin Bowen Payne (A.B. Payne). Pip was the dog, Squeak the penguin and Wilfred the young rabbit. It is believed that A. B. Payne's batman during the war had been nicknamed "Pip-squeak" and this is where the idea for the names of the dog and penguin came from. For some reason the three names of the characters became associated with the three campaign medals being issued at that time to many thousands of returning servicemen, and they stuck.

The 1914 Star

Established in April 1917

Also known as '*Pip*' or the '*Mons Star*'

This bronze medal award was authorized by King George V in April 1917 for those who had served in France or Belgium between 5th August 1914 to midnight on 22nd November 1914 inclusive. The award was open to officers and men of the British and Indian Expeditionary Forces, doctors and nurses as well as Royal Navy, Royal Marines, Royal Navy Reserve and Royal Naval Volunteer Reserve who served ashore with the Royal Naval Division in France or Belgium.

A narrow horizontal bronze clasp sewn onto the ribbon, bearing the dates '5th AUG. - 22nd NOV. 1914' shows that the recipient had actually served under fire of the enemy during that period. For every seven medals issued without a clasp there were approximately five issued with the clasp.

Recipients who received the medal with the clasp were also entitled to attach a small silver heraldic rose to the ribbon when just the ribbon was being worn.

The reverse is plain with the recipient's service number, rank, name and unit impressed on it.

It should be remembered that recipients of this medal were responsible for assisting the French to hold back the German army while new recruits could be trained and equipped. Collectively, they fully deserve a great deal of honour for their part in the first sixteen weeks of the Great War. This included the battle of Mons, the retreat to the Seine, the battles of Le Cateau, the Marne, the Aisne and the first battle of Ypres. There were approximately 378,000 1914 Stars issued.

The 1914-15 Star

Established in December 1918
Also known as *'Pip'*

This bronze medal was authorized in 1918. It is very similar to the 1914 Star but it was issued to a much wider range of recipients. Broadly speaking it was awarded to all who served in any theatre of war against Germany between 5th August 1914 and 31st December 1915, except those eligible for the 1914 Star. Similarly, those who received the Africa General Service Medal or the Sudan 1910 Medal were not eligible for the award.

Like the 1914 Star, the 1914-15 Star was not awarded alone. The recipient had to have received the British War Medal and the Victory Medal. The reverse is plain with the recipient's service number, rank, name and unit impressed on it.

An estimated 2.4 million of these medals were issued.

The British War Medal, 1914-18

Established on 26th July 1919
Also known as *'Squeak'*

The silver or bronze medal was awarded to officers and men of the British and Imperial Forces who either entered a theatre of war or entered service overseas between 5th August 1914 and 11th November 1918 inclusive. This was later extended to services in Russia, Siberia and some other areas in 1919 and 1920.

Approximately 6.5 million British War Medals were issued. Approximately 6.4 million of these were the silver versions of this medal. Around 110,000 of a bronze version were issued mainly to Chinese, Maltese and Indian Labour Corps. The front (obv or obverse) of the medal depicts the head of George V.

The recipient's service number, rank, name and unit was impressed on the rim.

The Allied Victory Medal

Also known as 'Wilfred'

It was decided that each of the allies should issue their own bronze victory medal with a similar design, similar equivalent wording and identical ribbon.

The British medal was designed by W. McMillan. The front depicts a winged classical figure representing victory.

Approximately 5.7 million victory medals were issued. Interestingly, eligibility for this medal was more restrictive and not everyone who received the British War Medal ('Squeak') also received the Victory Medal ('Wilfred'). However, in general, all recipients of 'Wilfred' also received 'Squeak' and all recipients of 'Pip' also received both 'Squeak' and 'Wilfred'.

The recipient's service number, rank, name and unit was impressed on the rim.

The Territorial Force War Medal, 1914-1919

Instituted on 26th April 1920

Only members of the Territorial Force and Territorial Force Nursing Service were eligible for this medal. They had to have been a member of the Territorial Force on or before 30th September 1914 and to have served in an operational theatre of war

outside the United Kingdom between 5th August 1914 and 11th November 1918. An individual who was eligible to receive the 1914 Star or 1914/15 Star could not receive the Territorial War Medal.

The obverse (front) of the medal shows an effigy of King George V with the words GEORGIVS BRITT OMN:REX ET IND: IMP:

The reverse of the medal has the words TERRITORIAL WAR MEDAL around the rim, with a laurel wreath and the words inside the wreath FOR VOLUNTARY SERVICE OVERSEAS 1914-1919.

Approximately 34,000 Territorial Force War Medals were issued.

The Silver War Badge

The Silver War Badge was issued on 12th September 1916. The badge was originally issued to officers and men who were discharged or retired from the military forces as a result of sickness or injury caused by their war service. After April 1918 the eligibility was amended to include civilians serving with the Royal Army Medical Corps, female nurses, staff and aid workers.

Around the rim of the badge was inscribed "For King and Empire; Services Rendered". It became known for this reason also as the "Services Rendered Badge". Each badge was also engraved with a unique number on the reverse, although this number is not related to the recipient's Service Number. The recipient would also receive a certificate with the badge. The badge was made of Sterling silver and was intended to be worn on the right breast of a recipient's civilian clothing. It could not be worn on a military uniform.

There were about 1,150,000 Silver War Badges issued in total for First World War service.

Awards

D.C.M. The Distinguished Conduct Medal ranks below the Victoria Cross and above the Military Medal for Non Commissioned Officers ('other ranks') See Cpl. H. L. Bavington D.C.M. These have *London Gazette* citations.

M.C. The Military Cross was designed to be a lesser award than the V.C. and was awarded to Captains and commissioned officers of lower grades. See Capt. C. Weare M.C. These also have *London Gazette* citations.

The Memorial Plaque was the name given to the bronze 121 mm. plaque which was sent to the next of kin of all who lost their lives on War Service. This was encased in a cardboard envelope and contained a message from the King and separately was sent a 'scroll' in a cardboard tube with the name, rank and unit of the deceased on it.

DCM

MC

Memorial Plaque

Abbreviations

Beds. and Herts.	Bedfordshire and Hertfordshire Regiment
B.E.	British Expeditionary Force
Bde.	Brigade
Bn.	Battalion
C.O.	Commanding Officer
Cpl.	Corporal
C.W.G.C.	Commonwealth War Graves Commission
D.C.M.	Distinguished Conduct Medal
D.S.O.	Distinguished Service Order
Div.	Division
D.O.W.	Died of Wounds
G.N.R.	Great Northern Railway
H.M.A.T.	His Majesty's Australian Troopship
H.M.S.	His Majesty's Ship
K.I.A.	Killed in Action
L.I.	Light infantry
M.C.	Military Cross
M.M.	Military Medal
M.G.C.	Machine Gun Corps
O.R's.	Other ranks
P.O.W.	Prisoner of War
Pte.	Private
R.A.M.C.	Royal Army Medical Corps
R.F.A.	Royal Field Artillery
R.G.A.	Royal Garrison Artillery
Sgt.	Sergeant
T.F.	Territorial Force
T.R.	Training Reserve
V.C.	Victoria Cross
Y.S. Bn.	Young Soldiers Battalion

Sources

Details from Hitchin War Memorial
Admission Register from Hitchin British Boys' School (1874-1914) and log books
Hitchin Museum's Newspaper Archives, The Hertfordshire Express and The North Hertfordshire Mail
Information from families of the soldiers
The Tank Museum, Bovington, Dorset

Internet sources

'Lest we Forget'
(http:www.roll-of-honour.com/Hertfordshire/Hitchin.html)
The Commonwealth War Graves Commission — http:www.cwgc.org
Ancestry — http:www.ancestry.co.uk
Regimental Museums
Regimental War Diaries
The Bedfordshire Regiment in the Great War transcribed by Steven Fuller — http:www.bedfordregiment.org.uk
National Archives — http://www.nationalarchives.gov.uk
The Library and Archives of Canada in Ottawa — http://www.collectionscanada.gc.ca
The National Archives of Australia in Canberra — http://www.naa.gov.au
The Imperial War Museum — http://www.iwm.org.uk
The Long, Long Trail — http://www.1914-1918.net
The Great War Forum — http://www.1914-1918.invisionzone.com
The Battle of Coronel website
The Great War Medals — http://www.greatwar.co.uk

Bibliography

The Order of Battle of Divisions by Major A.F.Becke R.F.A. 1, 2a,2b,3a,3b.
(published by Ray Westlake, Military Books 1935)
Pen and Sword Military Book series:
Ypres; Passchendaele, Polygon Wood, Sanctuary Wood and Hooge, Hill 60.
The Somme; Courcelette, Serre, Pozières, Delville Wood, La Boiselle.
The Hindenburg Line; Cambrai, Bourlon Wood, Flesquières.
French Flanders; Loos, Hill 60, Fromelles
British Regiments 1914-1918 by Brigadier E.A. James (pub. by Naval and Military Press1998)

The Somme Day by Day by Chris McCarthy (pub. by Arms and Armour Press 1993)

Passchendaele Day by Day by Chris McCarthy (pub. by Arms and Armour Press 1995)

Before Endeavours Fade by Rose Coombs M.B.E. (pub. by Battle of Britain International Ltd. 1976)

The Great War Medal Collector's Companion by Howard Williamson (Private Publishing 2011)

British Battalions on the Somme by Ray Westlake (pub. by Pen and Sword Select 1994)

The 24 Hour Trench by Andrew Robertshaw (pub. by The History Press 2012)

Battlefield Guides to the Ypres Salient and The Somme by Major and Mrs. Holt (pub. by Pen and Sword 1997)

The Battles of the Somme, A Topograghical History by Gerald Gliddon (pub. by Sutton Publishing 1998)

A Military Atlas of the First World War by Arthur Banks (pub. by Heinemann Educational Books Ltd. 1975)

Tommy by Richard Holmes (pub. by Harper Collins 2004)

Two minutes to the Station by Valerie Taplin and Audrey Stewart (pub. by Hitchin Historical Society 2010)

Hitchin's Century of Sacrifice by David Baines (privately pub;ished 1996)

Gordon Hall's personal library of Divisional Histories

'Comrades in Arms' a soldier's humour (author's collection)

An injured soldier's artwork in a nurse's autograph book copied from 'Fragments from France'

INDEX

Known Unto God

Beneath this foreign soil lies one,
*   christened by proud parents,*
*   welcomed by God*
*   and reared to respect.*

All too soon he was taken:
*   called by Kitchener,*
*   compelled by conscience,*
*   or committed by patriotism?*

With bible and pay book as close companions,
*   he sensed adventure,*
*   strove to please,*
*   and rapidly realised manhood.*

Under starry skies on lonely watch, he questioned;
*   "Where are you now Lord?"*
*   In your firmament,*
*   or in their trenches?*

At battle-pending drumhead service,
*   to the cross he turned*
*   and like Christ he craved*
*   courage and deliverance.*

Ignominiously now he lies beneath this foreign soil.
*   Respected by all.*
*   Remembered by few,*
*   but 'Known unto God'.*

Jean M. Bingham-Handley 2004